PÁDRAIG HARRINGTON'S
JOURNEY TO THE OPEN

www.**rbooks**.co.uk

TRANSWORLD PUBLISHERS
61–63 Uxbridge Road, London W5 5SA
A Random House Group Company
www.rbooks.co.uk

First published in Great Britain in 2007 by **Bantam Press** an imprint of Transworld Publishers

A CIP catalogue record for this book is available from the British Library.

ISBN 9780593060988

Addresses for Random House Group Ltd companies outside the UK can be found at:
www.randomhouse.co.uk
The Random House Group Ltd Reg. No. 954009

The Random House Group Limited supports The Forest Stewardship Council (FSC), the leading international forest-certification organization. All our titles that are printed on Greenpeace-approved FSC-certified paper carry the FSC logo.

Our paper procurement policy can be found at **www.rbooks.co.uk/environment**

Typeset in Goudy Old Style

Printed and bound in Great Britain by Butler and Tanner, Frome, UK

2 4 6 8 10 9 7 5 3 1

Every effort has been made to obtain the necessary permissions with reference to copyright material, both illustrative and quoted. We apologize for any omissions in this respect and will be pleased to make the appropriate acknowledgements in any future edition.

The images reproduced on pages 25 (inset), 29, 31, 32, 33 and 34 were kindly supplied by the Pádraig Harrington Charitable Foundation, the GUI and Stackstown GC. The image reproduced on page 21 appears courtesy of Alan Bleakley.

Unless otherwise stated, photographs for this book have been supplied by kind permission of Getty Images.

PÁDRAIG HARRINGTON'S
JOURNEY TO THE OPEN

with
Colm Smith
Dermot Gilleece
Karl MacGinty
Charlie Mulqueen
Brian Keogh
and
Philip Reid

BANTAM PRESS

LONDON · TORONTO · SYDNEY · AUCKLAND · JOHANNESBURG

To my dad

ACKNOWLEDGEMENTS

I would like to sincerely thank everyone who has helped
me along the road to this point in my career.

This book is for those who have played an active part in my
career development and in Irish golf. You know who you are and
this is your time to savour your contribution in helping me
become Open champion. Thanks to you all.

I would like to give personal thanks to those who have contributed
to this book, notably the journalists Greg Allen, Dermot Gilleece, Brian Keogh,
Karl MacGinty, Charlie Mulqueen, Philip Reid and Colm Smith,
for their time and expertise. Also to Getty Images, who have supplied
the vast majority of the photographs in the book, and the publishers,
Transworld, who took on the project at short notice.

Finally, I would like to thank everyone who has bought this book,
generating funds for very worthy causes.

For more information on Pádraig Harrington and his Charitable Foundation,
see his website at:

www.padraigharrington.com

Contents

Foreword

In the immediate aftermath of his historic win at Carnoustie, Pádraig, choking back the tears, mumbled, 'It's been a long, hard road.' How apt those words were!

This is the story of one of life's perennial workers, winding its way from the abject disappointment of a fourteen-year-old contesting his first tournament (Connacht Boys, play-off defeat – thanks, Gerald Sproule!) to the thirty-five-year-old Champion Golfer for 2007.

That he achieved one of his lifelong ambitions at Carnoustie was all the more remarkable considering that the last time he competed at the famed links we both looked into the abyss and never dared dream that it would repay Pádraig in spades. It was 1992, the British Amateur Championship; Pádraig was on fire and I was, as usual, caddying for him. He was hitting the ball with supreme confidence, his short game was in 'it doesn't matter where you put me' mode, and it was love at first sight with the rugged links. It was set up for him – tough, very tough, and tougher still! All went well until the last sixteen where we met a young Scotsman called Stephen Dundas. As in any tournament, not everything goes to plan, and we found ourselves two down early on. I kept on Pádraig's case, he kept grinding, and he got it back to all square by the 18th, one of the toughest holes in golf. Playing downwind, he hit a career drive down the right-hand side leaving just a six iron to the green. Dundas was in the left rough and had to lay up. A par four looked a winner. One flyer later, Pádraig was over the back of the green and out of bounds, out of the tournament, and out of his mind. We stood there, just the two of us, speechless.

Pádraig never ever made things easy for himself. There were other bitter disappointments along the way: the 1994 Irish Close Championship loss at Portmarnock to David Higgins, and the 1990 Irish Youths loss at Dundalk to David Errity. The phrase 'snatching defeat from the jaws of victory' springs to mind! But three Walker Cups and an impeccable record playing for Ireland made it an amateur career to savour. He signed off in the unpaid ranks with a memorable win at the Irish Close Championship played at Lahinch.

I finished my caddying career with Pádraig at the 1995 Tour School. I will never forget that week; wild horses wouldn't take me back there again! At the pre-qualifying event in Saint Cyprian, France, both of us actually saw a ghost. We were heading to the first tee in the last round when a player approached us who had just finished, and you could see straight through him he was that pale – Tour School has that effect on players, let me assure you. To all those players who have stepped up to the Tour School plate and failed, I applaud you. There are no parachutes or safety nets, just a yawning black hole, similar to the one we fatefully visited fifteen years ago at Carnoustie.

Now for something unusual: Pádraig cruised through Tour School and I said goodbye to his bag. It's a decision I have never regretted! We are still not just brothers, but also best friends. Fortunately, he won early in his professional career – his tenth event, the 1996 Spanish Open – and the rest, as they say, is history.

I have witnessed first hand how Pádraig goes about his business, working extremely hard and leaving nothing to chance. He is gutsy, determined, and deserves everything he achieves in the game. Ben Hogan had a reputation of being the purest ball striker in the game. When pressed for his 'secret', the man from Dublin in Texas said, 'It's in the dirt.' This philosophy – that diligence and hard work will reap rewards – is the mantra Pádraig has always lived by. Crucially, he still aspires to be the best player he can be.

As five brothers we all played the game and there is no doubt our competitiveness rubbed off on Pádraig. Through perseverance, he quickly became the best among us, showing those characteristics he still has today. Away from the public glare his practice rate is astonishing. His insatiable appetite for the game still reminds me of that five-year-old running around Stackstown with a club in his hand. We are all very proud of our little brother's achievements.

Finally, when I met Pádraig with the Claret Jug, he said, 'Look at the famous names on the trophy: 2005 – Tiger Woods, 2006 – Tiger Woods, 2007 – Tiger Harrington's brother!' He's that type of down-to-earth guy even today, and I know that our father, Paddy, would have been so proud.

To the readers, enjoy the journey! And to all you players, aspire!

Tadhg (Tiger) Harrington
October 2007

Prologue

CARNOUSTIE, SUNDAY, 22 JULY, 6.12 P.M.

After I've holed out on the 72nd hole I take a quick look at the leaderboard behind the stand, but it feels like an eternity, everything is in slow motion. You can see it in my face – I feel like I've lost The Open. I am examining the names and numbers, and it's the first time I've even noticed Andres Romero. I had no idea he had been leading with a couple of holes to play. I didn't even know which Romero was playing that week, Andres or Eduardo.

Emotionally down, I am spiralling, still trying to figure out what has happened, how the whole thing lies. And all the while I am succumbing to a terrible feeling of embarrassment. I have let myself down. I have let the fans down. I have let everybody down, it seems. It's a feeling that should have no place in my head or on a golf course. I spend a huge amount of my time working with my sports psychologist Bob Rotella on the whole idea that whatever happens during a round, it should not reflect on you. For me, though, the feeling of embarrassment is worse than failure, and it is beginning to overwhelm me.

There are many things going on in my head, but in reality it's only for a matter of seconds. These moments, though, are torture. At this stage I could descend very quickly into deep introspection because of the conflict within me. What an idiot I am; but how can I be an idiot? Logic has no place in this inner torment. I have probably played one of my best rounds of golf but messed up at the end; I have hit a couple of bad shots, but nobody's lost a life over it.

There's no holding back the sense of personal failure. It just won't go away. But then I see my son, Paddy, not quite four years old yet, running towards me. I can see his smiling face and it flicks a switch in me. Without thinking, I pick him up, and his delight, for all its innocence, stops my brooding in its tracks. I take maybe fifteen or twenty paces to leave the green and as I do so I wave to the crowds like I have just won The Open. It is such a pick-up at the right time because if I had let myself go any further emotionally downhill I would never have got back up for the play-off.

Even though I have just taken a double-bogey on the last hole of regulation play, my son thinks I'm a champion, which helps me put the situation into perspective and refocus for the play-off.

I walk off the green in exactly the same way as I stepped on to the 18th tee twenty minutes earlier, feeling as though I have just played the best golf of my life, feeling like a champion.

I never saw my drive bouncing off the bridge on the 18th, and in hindsight I'm so glad that it failed to make it across because if it had done so everyone would have said I was the luckiest Open champion in history. It is a semi-blind tee shot, so I just had to go by the oohs and aahs of the crowd, and there were enough of them for me to realize what had happened. Of course I was disappointed, but it was a tough shot, and walking down towards the Barry Burn near the 17th fairway I was still in a fairly optimistic state of mind.

That's when I saw Sergio walking towards me. He said hello and smiled. I was just looking at my target and trying to focus on what I was doing. I had gone into workmanlike mode. There wasn't anything for me to say, and I didn't want to get involved in a conversation.

After dropping under penalty, my disastrous third shot at the 72nd hole goes into the burn short of the green. In retrospect, I should have dropped further back in a better lie.

I had left myself 229 yards to the hole with out of bounds to the left and behind the green, while a right front bunker cut off a direct path to the flag. I could only aim at the front left portion of the putting surface, but that was guarded by the burn, which snaked across the fairway barely twenty yards short of the green. I chose to hit a five iron and with the wind down off the right I was very anxious not to go long.

There was also the issue of the grain of the grass lying against my ball, which heightened the possibility of a heavy contact. In retrospect, I should have gone back another fifteen yards where I could have dropped into a fairway lie, but that would have meant hitting a hybrid club or maybe a five wood on a right-to-left wind, which would have brought the out of bounds even more into play.

So when my third shot came out heavy and dribbled into the burn I started thinking, 'This is turning into a disaster,' and I felt disgusted. As I walked ahead Ronan, my caddie, implored me to stay focused. 'Let's play one shot at a time,' he said. 'Don't start getting into what it all means. We'll do the reflection afterwards.' His voice carried no emotion, and this is what he does best when he's at my side. He remains calm and constant whether I'm ten under par or ten over. It's like having

Bob Rotella out there with you. 'This isn't over yet,' he was insisting. 'Let's get up and down. Let's do our thing.' The conversation was a bit one-sided but it had its desired effect, and about fifty yards further down the fairway I had stopped dwelling on what had happened and was mentally getting into my next shot. Ronan had talked me back from being inwardly distraught to outwardly focused.

In the zone again, I looked around for the right place to take relief under penalty from the water hazard. Having made a critical dropping error after my tee shot, I now made up for it with the next decision. I spotted some grass where the mower blades had been lifted a little and opted to drop it there, barely four feet from the hazard, but I had a good stance and a good lie, forty-eight yards from the flag.

There were two obvious options. If I'd felt under pressure I would have played a pitch and run and hoped for the best through the bumps and hollows of the putting surface. For me, though, that option left too much to chance and a well-played shot might not have worked out as intended. Instead, what I had in mind was more difficult, but it was the one I knew would give me a great result if I

After dropping under penalty again, I am right back in the zone and play my fifth shot to the 72nd hole to five feet. The successful putt for double-bogey meant that Sergio needed a four to win the title.

executed it well. To do that, I had to be in a calm state of mind. Fortunately, Ronan's mini psychology lecture had already helped me regain my focus, so with a clear picture in my head of what I needed to do, I played an aggressive high-spinning pitch as routinely as I have ever played a golf shot. I felt no emotion standing over the ball. I could have been anywhere, in the smallest tournament, on the practice ground, or in my back garden.

As the ball travelled through the air, the crowd gave a collective 'ooh' as they thought it was long. But I knew better, although I expected the result to be a touch closer than it was. It skipped on its first bounce a little more than I'd anticipated before the spin on the ball bit into the green, and the crowd gave an 'aah' as it spun to a spot five feet beyond the hole. I enjoyed the crowd's surprise just like when I was a kid showing off to the members of Stackstown. I now had a difficult putt with enough left-to-right movement on it to make me feel tense and tight instead of loose and relaxed.

There were a lot of decisions to be made on the putt. If I aimed too far left, it would not come back enough on the break. If I tried to hit it in the middle of the hole it could veer off to the right. In the end it was a workmanlike putt, and with a very mechanical stroke, I holed it.

That's when I allowed myself to get emotionally involved in what had happened and what it all meant. Up to that point, all the way through the Championship, although I was convinced I would win, I never got emotionally involved. And then, just as the spiral downwards was threatening, my son bounded on to the green and the thoughts of 'I have just lost The Open by taking a six down the last' never got a look in. I just went to the recorders' hut, sat down and told myself, 'I am still in this tournament.'

As the name suggests, a recorders' hut is a fairly basic affair. There was a desk, a computer and very few items to distract either the player or the recording staff from their primary duties. This particular Portakabin did have a TV, but it was conspicuously switched off – conspicuous given the events that were unfolding barely a couple of hundred yards away as the final group, including the leader Sergio Garcia, was on its way down the 18th. It was obvious that the staff had read the situation, and just as I was making my entrance the TV had been turned off because images of how I had played the 18th were being replayed and trawled over by the commentators.

It was such a considerate and polite thing to do. But once I had signed my card and the paperwork was done, I asked them to switch it back on because I wanted to see what was happening. Sergio needed a par on the last to win, and, as I had just demonstrated, that was easier said than done. So they put the TV back on and one of the officials leaned over to put the sound up. I said, 'No, no, thanks.' I didn't need to hear the analysis of what I had just done, but I did need to see what the outcome was going to be.

I had already heard somewhere in the background that a commentator had said that the tee shot I struck on 18 was too aggressive. We will never know what the right play should have been, but Sergio subsequently proved that laying up short off the tee left an awful lot of work to make four. From 250 yards out, his approach shot found the left bunker, and from there he played a recovery shot to ten or twelve feet. As I watched, I was just trying to remain detached and neutral. I could not let myself get involved. The camera angle from behind his putter head showed that he struck a fine putt which had every chance of going in the hole. When it slipped by, Ronan and I stood up at exactly the same moment and both of us said, almost in unison, 'Let's go to work.'

We were met by Bob Rotella just outside and we all went to the putting green nearby. We asked about going to the range but the officials said no, the range wasn't open, and in any case we were going to be on the tee in five minutes.

At this stage I was only using up time. On the green, Paddy was chasing and deflecting my putts before they got to the hole so I spent more time chatting than practising. It was all quite casual and very relaxed, but I was becoming aware that I now had an advantage. I had dealt with my disappointment and I felt like I had come through it quite well. Sergio, meanwhile, had just suffered a setback of his own. And there was another big difference in the way the day had gone for both of us: in my mind I had played the better golf in shooting a 67 while he couldn't have been happy with the way he played in shooting a 73.

Bob told me two things as I was killing time. 'If you ever wanted to know that you have what it takes to win a major, that pitch shot on the last was all the evidence you need,' he said. 'If you can do that under those circumstances, you have it.' Then, as I headed to the 1st tee, he added, 'Let him focus on the result while you focus on the process.' It was a simple message, one that I can never be reminded of enough. Whether I had the edge or not, these two thoughts made me feel that I wasn't going to slip this time and I walked to the tee feeling as though I had the upper hand.

I was extremely positive about taking on four holes of a play-off, yet the most trepidation I felt all day was on that 1st tee again. My last two full swings had resulted in poor golf shots, and as I stood there, preparing to hit, I wasn't quite sure what to expect.

I went through my routine, struck a five wood, then looked up and watched my ball heading down the middle of the fairway. It was just a huge relief. I had made a good golf swing again, and it was business as usual. I felt hugely encouraged.

One thing I noticed as I was walking after the ball was that the temperature felt like it had dropped about ten degrees between the 18th hole and the play-off. After competing in the Irish PGA Championship the previous week on a links course, I remembered the difference that made to the flight of the ball. I strongly suspected that it would affect my clubbing for the approach shot, and with 162 yards to the pin I took out a seven iron, which I would normally hit up to eighteen yards further in warmer weather.

I wondered if Sergio had recognized the change in conditions. When his approach shot came up short in the bunker it confirmed my reasoning. So I stood there ready to play with the bit between my teeth. I was determined to make birdie, and I struck one of my most aggressive shots of the week. The pin was cut tight to the back right of the green but I fired my seven iron straight at it. As the ball was in the air, it looked perfect, and once the crowd cheered loudly I knew it was really good.

I now had a ten-foot putt on just about the same line as the eighteen-footer I'd had around five hours earlier. On that occasion I had aimed outside the left edge but it had stayed virtually straight. This time I just aimed at the left lip, but

After being given a second chance, the play-off starts and we cross the burn on our way down the first fairway. At this point I note that the temperature has dropped, which will affect our approach shots.

Using all my matchplay experience, I hole out for par on the second play-off hole to maintain my two-shot advantage.

it was funny, because even as I was lining up I felt as though I should have been allowing for more break. But I just had to trust the evidence of what I had seen earlier, and that crucial information helped me stroke it positively into the hole. My birdie against Sergio's bogey meant that I walked to the next tee with a two-shot lead.

As much as I felt a four-hole play-off would suit me, I couldn't help wishing now that it was just one hole of sudden death. But I had to banish those thoughts because Sergio was bound to respond with an aggressive shot on the par-three 16th, measuring 249 yards. I hit a safe shot using the right-to-left wind but it just drifted off the left side of the putting green. Sergio hit a really impressive long iron, holding it up into the wind; the ball struck the pin and bounced away to around eighteen feet.

For me, what happened next on that hole probably determined the outcome of the play-off. After I'd taken a two-shot advantage away from my good hole, he had fought back with a terrific golf shot from which he ultimately gained nothing. I made a good two-putt, he left his birdie effort short, and we both walked off the green with threes. It was like I was drawing on my experiences from every match I had ever played as an amateur, when I used to take the best any opponent could throw at me and then find some way of getting up and down to match or beat them. And there is no better feeling in head-to-head golf than knowing your opponent should have got something back off you but didn't. It must have been a body blow for him.

On the next, the par-four 17th, I could have taken a three-shot lead but I lost my focus. I hit a great tee shot and then a four iron, which I followed through the air with gritted teeth. The ball came to a stop just five feet from the hole. Sergio was twenty feet away but he made a great run at a difficult birdie putt and nearly holed it.

Then I faced up to that five-footer which, in my mind, would give me an insurmountable lead down the last. I knew the line, but I got ahead of myself thinking what a three-shot lead would mean and I tiddled it down the right side hoping for it to drop in. In fact, I never really got it on target. I missed it through a lack of intensity.

For a couple of seconds walking off that green I did lament my wishy-washy approach to that putt, but Ronan was like a broken record, prodding me verbally to stay focused. I still had a two-shot lead heading to the 18th tee, which was the fourth and final hole of the play-off.

One thing was for sure: the only way that Ronan would have taken the driver out of the bag was in two pieces. Hitting a three wood did not make sense either as I would have been hitting into the tightest past of the fairway. And there was another decision to be made that was critical: should I play it like a par four or a par five? Once I took my hybrid club out of the bag, I was taking the latter option, which I felt would force Sergio to make a three to keep the play-off alive. I felt some doubt standing over the hybrid as I hadn't hit that club off the 18th all week and I wasn't 100 per cent sure where the fairway was as it is somewhat concealed from where I was standing. I hit my shot on the same line as I had struck my driver less than an hour earlier, except this time it was sixty yards shorter and perfectly safe.

The next calculation to make was which club to use to lay up short of the Barry Burn. I had 210 yards to the hazard so I started to think that a five iron might not reach it. I thought to myself, 'I'll hit a six iron to be sure. No, let's take a seven iron, just to be doubly sure.' So I hit a very cautious lay-up well short of the water while Sergio, after driving into the left rough, hit a great recovery to thirty feet from the pin.

I go through my pre-shot routine before hitting my second shot to the third play-off hole to five feet. I miss my birdie chance but still walk off with a two-shot advantage.

I now had 103 yards left, which was just a smooth sand wedge. Right in the middle of my backswing I started to think, 'Don't hit it into the right-hand bunker.' And with that thought in mind, I hit a high floater which drifted a little too much on the wind and spun to the left before settling around thirty-five feet from the hole. It was not really what I was looking for. It was supposed to be no more than fifteen feet away.

Now I had a putt that I had to be careful with. All I was thinking was to roll it to the front edge and try to get it to fall in. After I stroked it, I thought it was perfect. It had a really good chance of going in, but it slid by. 'That's OK,' I thought to myself. 'It's only gone a foot by the hole . . . or two feet . . . oh no . . .' By the time it stopped rolling it was three and a half feet by. I knew there was a lot of work left in it. It was a bit of a shock.

As I watched Sergio prepare I tried to focus on my putt, but I did breathe a sigh of relief as his effort slipped by. He then holed a good five-footer for his four, and in hindsight I didn't mind because it would all have fizzled out if he had

missed. Now I was faced with my three-and-a-half-footer, and even though I normally dislike putts which break from right to left, at least there was no decision to be made about the line. I had seen the ball run past the hole and it broke a little, but not too much. It was inside right edge.

I drew the putter back and rolled it very smoothly. There was no effort or force in the stroke. It was as pure a putt as you could imagine. Once it was on its way, I looked up and saw the ball rolling end over end towards the middle of the hole. As good as the stroke was, I had never experienced so much doubt that a putt was actually going to drop until it physically disappeared. I was looking at it going in and thinking, 'Is it really going in?' 'Have I won The Open?' 'Is there any more golf today?' 'Is that it?' 'Does this mean I've won?' That putt was never going to miss, yet I doubted it right until the moment it dropped. I had to mentally pinch myself to prove that it was real.

My momentary confusion was not that surprising, I suppose, considering I had not at any stage during the day let my thoughts or emotions stray ahead to contemplate what winning would mean to me.

Amid the scenes of celebration after I holed out, I started doing the round of interviews. However, I realized then

Even though it never looked like it would miss, on the final green of the play-off I still can't believe that the ball is going to drop.

that I wouldn't be able to contain the emotions running through me for much longer. I had kept them in check until my putt had dropped; now there was no reason to hold them back.

Inevitably, I began to think about my dad. I thoroughly believed he had been out there with me all the time, but not once had I got involved in thinking, 'Gee, Dad, I could do with holing a putt here . . . are you watching me?' I just did not allow myself to think about him when I was on the course, so by the time it was all over those pent-up feelings rushed through me at double the speed and strength. I wasn't prepared for it. I tried to fight back the tears but I started choking up as I was speaking.

My dad would have deeply wanted me to win The Open, but he was very much a realist. He knew how hard it was to win one major, even if you were good enough. He would have been over the moon, but he had never made me feel in any shape or form that I had to succeed for him. He never lived his life through me and I never felt any pressure to please him. I felt he was on the green with me so I didn't feel sad that he wasn't there physically. It was funny in a way, because the week before at the Irish PGA Championship at the European Club in County Wicklow, I had really sensed his presence because of the informality of the galleries walking with the players on the fairways, just as he used to do in my amateur years.

I didn't see my mum for the four holes of the play-off, although she told me she was there all the way through. I would have forgiven her if she hadn't been able to watch. I'd also hardly seen my wife, Caroline – with the large galleries at The Open it is so difficult to pick someone out in the crowd. However, Paul (McGinley) made himself visible before I started the play-off. Miguel (Angel Jiménez) came out to the 1st tee, and although I knew he was out there for Sergio, he was very polite. We had been Ryder Cup partners as far back as 1999 and our encounter before the play-off was an illustration of the friendship we had built up over the years. He wished me luck and said at least we would have a European winner. To have Miguel and Paul out there, one Spaniard and one Irish guy, sort of evened it up in terms of support.

Eventually, things calmed down enough for the presentation ceremony to go ahead. When I lifted the Claret Jug it was funny, because I had been practising that move all day out on

I acknowledge the crowd, this time with the famous Claret Jug in hand. Among the many thoughts swirling around my head, my mind goes back to where it all started and all those who have contributed to my success.

the course. If you look at a replay, every time I raised my hand I was visualizing what it would be like to lift the trophy. When the moment came to do it for real, it was nice to experience what I had been visualizing all day and the feeling was everything I had imagined it would be.

As I turned around to take it all in, I could not help thinking of all those days as a boy in Stackstown I spent trying to hole 'this' putt to win The Open. I thought back to the practice I used to do, sometimes in appalling weather conditions. I would clear snow off the ground and strike ball after ball in wind, hail and such biting cold that if you thinned a shot you would cut the ball in two. Or at least that's how it felt.

I was hanging around Stackstown from around four years of age and had clubs cut down when I was seven, but I didn't really start playing seriously until I was nine. I took part in my very first competition when I was eleven, playing off a thirty-two handicap, and went out and won. I was thirteen when I played my first senior competition and won my class playing off nineteen. Then I got my handicap down and started playing in boys' tournaments, one of which, the Connacht Boys' Championship in Ballinasloe in 1986, whetted my appetite for competitive golf and remains clearly in my mind to this day.

I remember staying with a friend of my dad, Tom Morrisroe, and I turned up for my first practice round on my own. I was a bit homesick and I was out there playing away when this fourball came up behind me. Every time I looked round, there were two balls stone dead or at least close to the flag. By the time I got to the 18th I was totally dejected. I just wanted to go home. I thought I would never be good enough to play or compete with these guys. The interesting thing was that far from being inadequate that week, I somehow raised my game to play my very best golf and reach the final, where I came up against Gerard Sproule, who had been responsible for all those fine approach shots during my dispiriting practice round, having hit a number of approach shots to each hole.

Unfortunately, it all ended in tears. Having played so well for so long, I lost a ball on the fourth extra hole of sudden death. It was the only time I have ever cried after a round of golf. But whatever happened that day, even the good shots that didn't turn out well, it made me want more.

There's no doubt that while I was celebrating on the 18th in Carnoustie, posing for the cameras with the Claret Jug and taking in all that was going on around me, I spent a good deal of the time thinking about what it had taken to get to where I was. There is definitely a double standard within me. There's an inner voice that tells me, 'Wow, I can't believe I have got this far. I've never had the talent.' I know my own inadequacies, my own fears, and there are so many players over the years who I've thought were better than me. But there's another part of me that has incredible self-belief. That part of me feels that everything is possible because from a very young age I always felt that I had the ability, patience and stamina to figure things out. And that, I think, is my real talent – a capacity to work my way through a problem while never losing sight of the goal, and to find the information to keep developing. I've always said that I am a work in progress. I am not the kind of guy who has it all.

Even on the night before the final round of The Open I said to Bob Rotella, 'Bob, I've been thinking. What if we—'

Bob looked at me and simply said, 'I think you're in the right place right now. We'll leave that well enough alone.'

There were so many little things during the week of The Open that pointed to something special happening. Bob Rotella stayed with me, and it is very rare that he is there on the last day of a major. And the other Bob, my swing coach Bob Torrance, was honoured by the Association of Golf Writers on the Tuesday night earlier in the week, after sixty years' service to the game.

Bob and I have been working together since The Open at Birkdale in 1998. I learned quite quickly after turning professional that he was the best swing coach on Tour. Every player under Bob's wing struck the ball well. At the World Cup at Kiawah Island in 1997 I could see what he had done for my partner Paul McGinley because he was sublime from tee to green that week. I wanted to be like Paul.

The realization that I had to do something about my swing dawned on me in a big way at the US Open at the Olympic Club the following June. I finished in a tie for thirty-second place after chipping and putting my way around the course. With the condition of my long game at the time, there was no way I could have finished any higher. So I started working with Bob in the wind and gales of Birkdale the following month. For me it was a logical step to take: I had always sought out the best available people in their field to bring me on, like my physio Dale Richardson, my conditioning coach Dr Liam Hennessy, biomechanics expert Paul Hurrion and Bob Rotella.

Of course, my family, too, have always been there for me as a support network, and my wife Caroline is my closest confidante. She is the one I can talk to logically, and there is no one better at giving me a kick up the backside when I start sulking. But if I have a bad day and need a twenty-minute rant, she will sit there and listen. If she feels that I need to be told to stop feeling sorry for myself, she will tell me. After The Open, when I needed to take a break because of fatigue and an accumulation of injuries, she said to me, 'I can see it in your eyes. You're just not there.' She is the perfect pillar behind me. I know she is always in my corner no matter what happens.

Whatever competitive streak I have, I got from my mum. She is very determined and competitive, much more so than my dad was. She is quite black and white about things, and I could do with more of that.

The two ladies and two great influences in my life: my wife, Caroline, and my mum, Breda.

I think I got a little bit of all my brothers' traits. The eldest, Tadhg, has so much determination and guts, and I spent years with him when he was my caddie. Talk about an ability to over-achieve. He's incredible. The odd chance he would get to win he would just go ahead and do it, whereas I would need ten chances before I would actually take one.

My next eldest brother, Columb, is without question the most intelligent golfer of the five of us. He has a remarkable ability to think his way around a golf course. My middle brother, Fintan, is the least interested in the game but he has the best swing by far among us. Then comes Fergal, the closest to me in age and the one I played the most golf with growing up. He has a great love of the game and is a real enthusiast.

My dad, I think, was all five of us in one, and I got my fascination with developing my game from him. I think I also got all the parts in one bundle. I have a little of all of their strengths, so it must be true what they say: the youngest brother gets everything.

Golf is fickle. I have spent my whole life trying to realize that. I walked away from the 2007 Open celebrating my win. I have the trophy sitting on my breakfast table and I have my tea and toast around it. I get up every day at home and it's there. It is very easy to live with. But there isn't a day that goes by when I don't think about triumph's twin, failure. If Sergio's putt had gone in on the 18th first time round there would have been a lot of second-guessing about the way I had played the same hole and about the wisdom of my decision to hit the driver off the tee.

I know only too well that the difference between winning and losing is extremely small. The skill factor is in actually putting yourself in a position to win, and there are a lot of players who are not prepared to put their head on the line. You have to want to be out there. You have to want to be in the fray. Take the way I won the Order of Merit last year. I did what I could on the final day, but if Sergio had got up and down out of a bunker on the 18th in Valderrama, it would have been a different outcome. But I had done well to put myself in position, and sometimes the cards fall for you. It was a similar

situation in the Irish Open. If Bradley Dredge had birdied the par-five 18th at Adare, or the play-off hole, people would have been saying that I lost another event. I wouldn't have done anything differently so I have to take satisfaction in how I approached everything in the knowledge that I did the best I could.

Make no mistake, though. I love winning, and I make a special effort to celebrate a victory far more now than I would have several years ago. But it is almost as if the winning is for everyone else around me. The satisfaction is just for me.

My thoughts go back to my dad and everything he taught me and did for me, from the long hours spent on the practice ground to caddying for me.

So many memories and hard lessons learned along the path of my career whirled in and out of my head in those glorious minutes of celebration on the 18th green at Carnoustie. I don't think that any of my fellow competitors in my amateur days would have pointed to me and said that I was the guy who would go on and win The Open. I competed against all of the best players in Britain and Ireland and beat many of them through determination, but the ultimate satisfaction for me is how far I have progressed since then. I am happy, too, that I have not dwelt negatively on my failures to the point where they have become destructive. The Connacht Boys' Championship defeat, when I was just fifteen, gave me an appetite for the sharp end of competitive golf that I have to this day, and I recall that experience with great fondness.

But probably the most telling and relevant experience of all, in terms of my development mentally in competition, came at Dundalk Golf Club in the Irish Youths' Amateur Open Championship in 1990 when I was two shots clear with four holes to play. There were no scoreboards around, but when I got to the 15th tee I was informed that I was two shots ahead and I immediately began to believe I was going to win. Far from feeling any nerves, I lost all of my intensity and bogeyed three of the last four holes to be overtaken by the eventual winner, David Errity. I know that a number of players called me a 'choker', but in fact the opposite had happened. I had lost my intensity, and that is something I still have to fight against. It happened again at Carnoustie when I missed that short putt on the third play-off hole, but my experience helped me spot it and I refocused for the tee shot on the last hole. Who would have thought that bogeying three of the last four holes would help me win The Open seventeen years later, although there are a lot of experiences over the years that have helped to make me the golfer that I am.

A lot of people have asked me how disappointed I felt after missing out on The Open play-off by a single stroke at Muirfield in 2002. That really didn't hurt me that much, although I was very disappointed at the time. The key there was that I did not think I was going to win because Ernie Els was three shots clear. So I took the driver out on the 18th, trying to force another birdie, and it didn't come off. Nobody could have predicted that six under was going to get into the play-off. It is so much harder to deal with defeat when you feel you deserve to win. But it's true what they say about such experiences being the ones you learn the most from, even the ones that hurt deeply.

Probably the hardest loss I've had to deal with, and the only time I have ever been truly angry after a defeat, was the Irish Close Championship final in 1994 at Portmarnock, where I had been two up with three to play against David Higgins but lost by three-putting the second play-off hole. I took it very badly. I was in the car park afterwards with my dad and I was trying to kick my clubs into the boot. I was twenty-two years old, and the only reason I wasn't crying was because I was so annoyed. If I hadn't got the clubs into the car I would have been jumping on them. I could have broken every one of them. And it was no reflection on David. You could not lose to a nicer guy, but that didn't ease the pain. I needed something to take away from it. I had been in a commanding position but I hadn't won.

In retrospect, that setback and what followed was typical of the ebb and flow of my career. I have never found it easy to get to the next level until I have served my time and achieved at the step below. And that often means encountering and dealing with adversity and defeat. As it turned out, I did take something away from losing that day because the following year I won both the Irish Close and Strokeplay Championships.

As I stood by the boot of the car that day at Portmarnock, my dad didn't so much try to console me as listen to my anger and angst. When he eventually said something, it was a simple message, and the only thing that made any sense in that situation. I can still hear him saying it.

'There will be better days, son, there will be better days.'

Pádraig Harrington
October 2007

A dream comes true as I am presented with the Claret Jug and announced as 'Champion Golfer of the Year'.

CHAPTER ONE: 1976–1995
Clubbing together

Colm Smith

The story starts at Stackstown, set in the hills above Dublin city, where the then Garda Commissioner, Edmund Garvey, acquired acreage on some of the most rugged land imaginable, his intention to build a sports complex for the exclusive use of the Garda Síochána. That idea was later changed by some wise men who had the foresight to build a golf course.

Among the group was one Paddy Harrington, a Cork Garda who had relocated to Dublin. His first sporting love was unquestionably Gaelic football, at which he was a star performer for his native county, reaching two All-Irelands but losing both. Next on his list of leisure activities was golf, at which he was also adept. The youngest of his five sons, Pádraig, is the current holder of the Open Championship, the highest accolade the game has to offer. Had it not been for men like his dad, Paddy Power, Denis Devine, Jim Mahony, Jim McGuane, Dan Buggy, Patsy O'Donnell and others, however, the young Harrington's chosen sport might just as easily have been football or hurling, both of which he played at Coláiste Éanna in Rathfarnham. He may even have continued with accountancy, which was his chosen career after his school days. Sadly, Paddy passed away just two years before Pádraig proudly paraded the coveted Claret Jug around the 18th green at Carnoustie in July 2007, only the second Irishman (after Fred Daly in 1947) in the 136-year history of the event to hold the title. There was surely time for a tear in memory of the man who made it possible.

Some 140 acres of rubble, rocks and stones had to be cleared from the mountainous site. There was no machinery. The greens and fairways were fashioned – they call it shaping nowadays – by manual labour, men and boys

Pádraig and his brother Tadhg line up a putt at Portmarnock during the 1991 Walker Cup. Long-term caddie Tadhg remained on the bag until Pádraig earned his European Tour card in 1995.

stamping on the sand to level the greens. Pádraig and his four brothers were involved as well. 'When I was five,' Pádraig recalls, 'there must have been fifty or more people out there. We were in wellies and we were just told to go out there and tramp on the greens. My brothers were out there too but they were older and had to pick up stones from the ninth and eighteenth fairways on their hands and knees.' He laughs heartily at the thought. 'I was the privileged one . . .'

It was a real community effort that came to fruition in 1976; affiliation to the Golfing Union of Ireland (GUI) followed. The spacious clubhouse was built five years later and officially opened by Gareth Fitzgerald, the former Irish Taoiseach. It boasts stunning views of the city and Dublin Bay from Howth to Bray. Not only was he a co-founder, Paddy also served as president, captain and committee man.

There was a great bond between all the Harrington family members, and all of them played golf. 'My dad took up golf when he retired from [Gaelic] football after reaching two All-Ireland finals with Cork,' Pádraig says. 'He was a very intelligent golfer. His lowest handicap was four and he won forty-four prizes off that handicap. He played at Slade Valley Golf Club for a few years before Stackstown opened in 1976. He used to hit the ball miles, but it was all over the place. So he took it upon himself to change his swing to hit the ball straighter. He figured it out himself and began to hit the ball shorter but much straighter. I have a lot of my dad's traits as far as golf is concerned. He was always trying to get better for next week. I also have a lot of my dad's psyche, and sometimes I worry about that because I'm not hard enough. But I'm getting there.

'While Dad probably had the greatest influence, all my family – my four brothers and my mum – contributed. Tadhg was a huge influence. He caddied for me through most of my amateur career, right up to when I turned pro. My dad also caddied quite a bit. I got more of my competitiveness from Tadhg and my mum while I inherited more of my will to keep improving from my dad. My dad didn't like flying at all because he used to suffer badly with his ears in the air and he would get a bit disoriented for a day or two, so he didn't travel out of the country very much. One thing about him was that he never needed to live his sporting life through me, like many other parents. He never made me feel I had to do something for him. There was never a question of me having to play golf for my dad. I never had to win for him to be proud.'

Pádraig's mother, Breda, also plays at Stackstown, and they had the pleasure of playing together on a number of occasions in the former Flogas Mother and Son tournament, once finishing second in a field of 159 pairs in an All-Ireland final at Malahide, beaten by just half a point.

Pádraig pictured with mum, Breda, who caddied for him during the par three contest prior to the Masters at Augusta in 2006.

Unsurprisingly, at an early age Pádraig really started to get interested in golf. 'I remember at five years of age somebody giving me a club,' he continues. 'I don't actually recall who it was, probably one of my brothers, but I remember it was an eight iron with a big chunk out of the grip. The club was too long for me of course, but I kept trying for years in the back garden. I still have the club.

'When I was seven I got three clubs cut down for my birthday – a three, a five and a seven iron. I actually lost the three iron when I was out rooting for lost balls. I disturbed a wasps' nest at the bottom of a tree and got stung. Fergal was with me and we ran like mad, and I dropped the club. I went back the following day to collect it but it was gone. I was heartbroken – not about the sting but about the club.

'From the age of nine I spent all my summers in Stackstown. I wasn't allowed to become a member until I was eleven because of insurance reasons, but I still played and practised on the course. Once I reached eleven, I joined the club with a thirty-two handicap and won my first boys' competition, although I'm not sure if I won the overall or just my class.'

By the time he was thirteen it was obvious that a latent talent was about to emerge. Pádraig won his first senior competition at the club off a handicap of nineteen, and that same year he began to play in the inter-club junior competitions, his handicap dropping with remarkable alacrity: at the age of thirteen he went from nineteen to fourteen; at fourteen to a nine; by fifteen he had reached five; at sixteen he had got down to one; and from seventeen to scratch – a drop of nineteen shots in four years! Interestingly, he had few formal lessons during that time. 'My first ever lesson was with Bangor professional Davy Jones, who was with the GUI at the time when I was fifteen or sixteen,' Pádraig says. 'Then I worked for the next ten years with Howard Bennett, the GUI's new national coach, who helped develop my short game and character into much of what you see today. A better role model you could not find. But I must say that when at home, if I wasn't playing well, I would always go to Wattie Sullivan, the professional at The Grange Golf Club in Dublin.'

If you listen to or read about Pádraig recalling his teenage days, it may seem like his only interest was golf. He was, in fact, an all-round sports kid. 'I played Gaelic football and hurling all the way through school at Ballyroan Boys' National School and Coláiste Éanna secondary school, and also for the club Ballyboden St Endas, all of which were close to my home. I also played soccer for Broadford Rovers and Newbrook Celtic, and a bit of basketball. I played three matches each weekend and was goalkeeper for all three. I was actually a pretty good hurler, better at that than football.' Golf simply had to be fitted into the schedule.

As he got older and improved, the demands were greater. 'I gave up hurling at fourteen, and when I was sixteen I was picked for the Leinster Youths' golf team for

1988 Irish Boys' team
for the European Boys'
Team Championship in
Renfrew, Scotland.
Back row (*left to right*):
Bobby Kinsella, Paul
Russell, Gary McNeil,
Declan Cunningham.
Front row (*left to right*):
Stuart Paul, Dick Perry
(captain), John McKornan,
Pádraig Harrington.

the interprovincials at Massereene in county Antrim. The team was to go north for a day's practice, but it clashed with my last game of football for Coláiste Éanna in the final of the Dublin Colleges Championship. It was a very important game for me because the match was in Croke Park and I was captain. Mick McGinley, Paul's father, was Leinster golf captain and I had to get special permission not to travel with the team. The last thing Mick said to me was, "Don't get injured."

'I would normally have played goal full-back, but this time they put me in at centre-back to mark a guy called Dessie Farrell from St Vincent's, Glasnevin. He was a short guy and didn't look to be up to much. But did I get a lesson, and more? He goes, he's fast, and I go with him. The pitch was hard and wet and I slipped, put my hand down and sprained my left wrist. He just ran rings around me that day. The same Dessie Farrell, of course, became one of Dublin's best players and won an All-Ireland medal in 1995. For the record, we lost the match 2–9 to 0–5, but it is still a very special memory.

'I got my wrist bandaged up and made my way to Massereene. When I got to the hotel I didn't see anyone else around so I went to bed. I came down the following morning for breakfast with my arm strapped up and I said I'd just fallen in the bedroom. I couldn't tell him I'd sprained it in the match. No one took much notice, but I could hardly hold the club with my left hand and I could only hit the ball about 220 yards. I was just hitting it with my right hand, just guiding it. I don't think the captain knew just how bad the pain was, because I was able to hide it, and I hadn't the guts to tell him. Would you believe that I sprained it so badly that I still get treatment on it to this day?'

Pádraig's soccer career also ended around that time. 'A man called Sean Reeves from Broadford took me for a trial with Dublin County. I was to go in goal for fifteen minutes, but within thirty seconds I got a pass back and I let it through my legs. I had to stand there for another fourteen and a half minutes knowing it was a pointless exercise. He encouraged me to stay, but I knew this was the end of my soccer career. Being a goalkeeper is a tough job. I was pretty good at it, but I was also prone to the odd blunder.'

No matter: by this time Pádraig's sights were firmly focused on golf. 'I preferred golf for the fact that I was in control of my own destiny,' he says. His first official tournament was the Connacht Boys' Championship at the age of fifteen. He lost in the final at the twenty-second hole of sudden death and was absolutely inconsolable. However, it wasn't all bad news, 'My brother Tadhg caddied for me that day, and it was the start of many happy years together on the amateur circuit.'

Pádraig soon put that reverse behind him when he was picked for the Irish Boys' Home International Championship at Kilmarnock Barassie in Scotland; and the year of 1988 was another milestone in his blossoming career: he was runner-up to Damien McGrane in the Irish Boys' at Birr and won the Leinster Boys' title, his first official victory, at Royal Tara by an amazing eleven shots. His mother Breda, as many people know, is a devoted supporter, and Royal Tara was the first time she had watched her son play competitive golf. 'I had this shot to a long par three,' Pádraig remembers. 'I hit it towards the right side of the green in a left-to-right wind and I'm shouting, "Hook, hook, hook!" My mother thought I was shouting something not dissimilar, and she nearly had to be restrained from dragging me off the golf course!'

It was a very busy year for the young star, with three major international events also on the schedule. Formby in England was the venue for both the Great Britain and Ireland (GB&I) match against the Continent of Europe (which the home side won), and the Home Internationals, which England won. The European Team Championship followed, played at Renfrew in Scotland. It was won by France. They weren't exactly great occasions for Ireland, but Pádraig put in some very satisfactory individual performances: he won both his singles against the Continent of Europe, won three out of four in the Home Internationals, and five out of six in the European Team Championship – a total of ten wins from a possible twelve. 'If you want to know the difference between the haves and the have-nots,' Pádraig says,

'I caddied for Gary McNeill in a GB&I Boys' match against Europe and the guy he was playing had this set of beryllium Ping irons with graphite shafts that must have been worth around £2,000 [Irish punts at the time]. For my first Home Internationals I owned a half-set of imitation Ping Eye irons that cost £110, and I borrowed the other half from my brother. So the whole set cost £110!'

Nineteen eighty-nine was another successful year on the individual front, Pádraig winning both his singles in the Home Internationals and five out of six matches in the European Team Championship in Sweden; both competitions were won by England. He also finished second in the Leinster Youths' Championship and third in both the Irish and Connacht Youths' Championships – all before passing his eighteenth birthday.

Amid that torrent of international golf fixtures in the late eighties, there was room for a little romance. Pádraig's wife Caroline tells the story. 'My dad Dermot [Gregan] was a member of Stackstown and he decided I should join. The first day he brought me up to show me round. There was a golf match on and, you know my dad, he's a big golf fan, and he suggested that I should watch. I said, "You must be joking." In any case, we watched, and Pádraig was playing with Kit Flood, his best friend and brother of Ronan, who now caddies for Pádraig and is married to my

1989 Irish Boys' team for the Home Internationals in Nairn, Scotland. Back row (*left to right*): J. Clarke, G. Sproule, C. Bell, G. Murphy, P. Harrington, R. Coughlan, D. Kyle, S. Parkhill. Front row (*left to right*): R. Burns, M. McGinley (manager), J. McKernan (captain), G. Deegan, M. Sinclair.

younger sister Susie. My dad introduced me to these prospective junior golf partners following their match, and before you know it, I have a date with Kit! He asked me first. He was a bit more brash than Pádraig. It only lasted about six weeks and Pádraig asked me out after that.'

But the match wasn't immediate. 'Funny thing was,' says Pádraig, taking up the story, 'Caroline saw me hit the best drive of my life and I still don't know how I hit it that far. It took me a few months before I asked her out. I suppose I was a bit shy about it. It's tough to go up to your best mate and ask him, "Is it all right if I ask out your ex-girlfriend?" But, "Not a problem," he said.'

Pádraig lines up to play Scotland's Jim Milligan in the 1990 Home Internationals in Wales, Pádraig's first appearance for the senior Irish team.

Caroline and Pádraig were married in 1997, two years after he turned pro. They have a four-year-old son called Patrick, after Pádraig's father.

Back in the early nineties, when he and Caroline were still courting, Pádraig realized it was time for his golf to move on, even though he was not exactly laden with age-group victories. In fact he had only two to his name: the 1988 Leinster Boys' title, and the Leinster Youths' in 1991, which he won by an equally superb ten shots. The two victories constituted the biggest winning margins ever produced in junior competition in Ireland. But Pádraig was generally there or thereabouts in other tournaments. (Much the same applied to his early performances at senior level for a number of years, when he became dubbed 'the nearly man'. It took him four years to notch up his first senior title.)

Pádraig regards 1990 as his breakthrough year. It started with an invitation from the Golfing Union of Ireland selectors to join the annual warm-weather training session in Quinta do Lago, Portugal. 'I was one of the junior members of the squad and there was a bit of banter from, shall we say, a couple of the elder statesmen. For instance, on the first tee, one asked, "Who are these young guys? Why are they here? They haven't proved anything." It was just the kind of challenge I thrive on, and I believe I lost only one match throughout the week.' There was also a fine

individual performance for Ireland in the first ever European Youths' Team
Championship, in Turin, with five wins from six matches.

Pádraig then reached the semi-final of the South of Ireland and the final
of the Irish Close at Baltray, losing each time to Darren Clarke, who won both.
The transition from junior to senior had brought Pádraig into the league of players
that included the likes of Clarke and Paul McGinley, with whom he was later to
make a significant impact during Europe's three consecutive Ryder Cup victories.
'Although I lost to Darren in the final I was very happy with one aspect of my
game: in the semi-final I beat Mark Gannon by out-chipping and -putting one
of the greatest short-game players on his home course.'

Pádraig was still without a major title, but these performances were good
enough to earn him a deserved place on the senior international team for the first
time. He celebrated in style by winning six out of six as Ireland won the Triple
Crown at Conwy GC, Wales, for the second time in four years. 'I was shocked
when the team was announced and captain George Crosbie put me in at number
three in the singles order. Let's face it, I was only a cub as far as the senior
internationals were concerned. I felt like it was the sacrificial lamb, and I said so
to George. But being the good captain that he was, he gave me great confidence
when he said that the reason he put me in there was because he knew I was good
enough to get the job done. Maybe it was a gamble as far as he was concerned, but
it paid off. I was drawn against Scotland's Jim Milligan, a Walker Cup player from
1989. I parred the first six holes and was a couple up, and I thought to myself, "This
isn't too bad." I went on to win all six matches and I never played lower than third
in the team after that. It was one of the highlights of my career, because in six
years playing for Ireland in the Home Internationals and the European Team
Championship I never lost a singles match.'

In 1991 Pádraig lost in the semi-final of the South of Ireland for the second
year in a row, this time to McGinley, who went on to win the title. Once again,
however, he won six out of six matches for Ireland in the European Team
Championship, in Madrid, and contributed handsomely to the Irish cause with
four and a half points from six as Ireland retained the Home International crown
at County Sligo. Ireland shared the title with England in 1992, at Prestwick GC,
Scotland. It was the last time a title was shared; from then on in the event of a tie
the result would be decided on a count-back of matches played. Garth McGimpsey,
a Royal Portrush specialist having won the North of Ireland title there five times,
including three in a row, beat Pádraig in the final in 1993, but he continued to do
well for Ireland that year, winning eight of his twelve matches between the Home
Internationals at Royal Liverpool (shared with England) and the European Team
Championship in the Czech Republic.

Pádraig pictured in his
Irish team blazer in the
Stackstown yearbook
of 1991.

The elusive major championship finally arrived over the Easter weekend in 1994 when Pádraig, at the age of twenty-one, won the West of Ireland on the County Sligo links at Rosses Point. It was particularly sweet because he seemed to be heading for another runner-up spot when he went four down after eight to former winner Ken Kearney; but, he recalls, 'Ken missed an eight-foot putt on the ninth and that spurred me on. I clawed my way back and won on the final hole. But I missed two other good chances to win later in the year. I lost both the South of Ireland and the Irish Close finals to David Higgins from Waterville. David beat me on the last hole at Lahinch and on the twentieth in the Close after being two up with three to play at Portmarnock. Both were bitter pills to swallow.'

Nineteen ninety-five was Pádraig's final year as an amateur, and it was undoubtedly his very best year. He reached four finals, winning two – and those two wins came in the most important events. 'I won the Irish Open Strokeplay Championship at Fota Island [the event had been revived after a lapse between 1960 and 1994], and later in the year I led the Irish Close qualifying round at Lahinch with a record 66, and beat Richie Coughlan 3&2 in the final.' Pádraig was the first player to hold the Close and Open Strokeplay titles at the same time since Joe Carr in 1954. The two finals he lost were the South of Ireland (to his Walker Cup partner Jody Fanagan, on the final

Pádraig pictured with Jody Fanagan, his foursomes partner on many Ireland and GB&I teams. Together they won twenty-two out of thirty matches representing both Ireland and GB&I.

hole) and the North of Ireland (to Keith Nolan, on the 19th). 'I broke seven course records between 1994 and 1995 and finished off the year winning eleven out of twelve matches playing for Ireland in the Home Internationals and European Team Championship,' Pádraig recalls.

He has always been extremely proud to play for Ireland. In total, Pádraig teed it up 114 times for his country at all levels and had a final strike rate of 72 per cent for all matches and 92 per cent for all singles played.

This sense of pride translated well to the Walker Cup arena. While many may have thought Pádraig was destined to turn professional when he was eighteen years old, he had no intention of doing so. 'It was at twenty-one I decided I would become a professional at twenty-four,' he says, 'based on the fact that I was beating everybody else who was turning pro. I didn't really think I was good enough, but if these guys thought they were good enough and I could beat them, then it had to be worth giving it a go. I finished my accountancy qualification when I was twenty-three, so I took a year off to play golf and see how it went.' Another big reason, he once admitted to me, was that he didn't want to leave the amateur ranks without having been in a winning Walker Cup side.

Pádraig plays an approach shot during the 1991 Walker Cup at Portmarnock in front of his home crowd, a match the home team lost 14–10.

Pádraig's first appearance in the Walker Cup was as part of the team that played against the Americans at Portmarnock in 1991. 'I had a great year to make the team,' he recalls, 'but to be truthful, I was a bit overawed by the occasion, having just celebrated my twentieth birthday. I played one foursomes the first day with Paul McGinley and we lost 2&1 to Allen Doyle and Jay Sigel, who was the most capped player in the history of the event with eight consecutive appearances [he made his ninth and last appearance two years later]. Doyle is one of the best golfers I have seen. I have never seen ball striking like it. In fact it was a pretty strong American team: apart from Doyle and Sigel they also had Phil Mickelson and David Duval. I played singles the second day and went three up after three on David Egar, but lost 3&2. In fairness, he played really well, but for me it was a disappointing loss. I was probably lacking a bit in experience. We lost 14–10.'

In 1993, the meeting between the countries produced an even greater loss. At Interlachen in Minnesota, the Americans won 19–5 – the greatest margin in the entire history of the event, which had started in 1922 at the National Golf Links in New York. GB&I had won only four times with one halved in thirty-three meetings up to 1995. Only once had they won on American soil, and that was at Peachtree in 1989 with a team that included two Irishmen, Eoghan O'Connell and Garth McGimpsey. Eoghan remained undefeated in the match. On the first day he won 6&5 in the foursomes (with Peter McEvoy) and 5&4 in the singles; on day two he and McEvoy halved the foursomes; then Eoghan scored a vital half point with Phil Mickelson.

At Interlachen, the first series of foursomes was washed out and it was decided to play all ten singles on each of the two days with one set of foursomes on the second morning; although it was something of a shambles as far as the visiting squad was concerned, with the selectors naming a ten-man squad with nine rookies. Pádraig was the only one with Walker Cup experience, and the oldest man on the squad

Pádraig putts during the 1993 Walker Cup matches at Interlachen, USA, which GB&I lost heavily 19–5.

was twenty-four-year-old Mat Standford. The Americans won six and halved one of the ten singles on the first day. They then won the four foursomes and eight of the ten singles, with one halved on the second day. Raymie Burns was the only winner, and Pádraig, who had been beaten in both singles and foursomes on day one, salvaged a half-point from his singles. 'Certainly it was our first time to experience the set-up of the American courses,' Pádraig observes, 'and most of the guys wouldn't have been used to the rough around the greens. I was comfortable enough with it. I played good golf, but all I got out of it was a half point from three matches. I was four or five up on Brian Gay but only came out with a half. It was very disappointing.'

At Royal Porthcawl two years later, however, he finally got his wish. 'There were two high points in my amateur career,' he says. 'One was winning the Triple Crown in 1990, and the other was winning the Walker Cup at Royal Porthcawl in 1995. I was inexperienced in 1991 and 1993 and I didn't do myself justice, so you could say that winning the Walker Cup meant a lot to me. We had a fantastic team. I would say that no Walker Cup team had been better prepared than for Royal Porthcawl. Clive Brown of Wales was the captain and you got the impression that no stone was left unturned to make sure that everything was right for the players.'

GB&I lost the foursomes on the first day 2½– 1½; Jody Fanagan and Pádraig were the winning pair. The afternoon singles saw a tremendous effort by the eight players: they won 5½ points and turned the tie around. Pádraig beat Jim Courville by two holes. Jody didn't play, but he was one of the stars of the show on the second day: Pádraig and he had a stunning 2&1 victory over John Harris and Tiger Woods, as the foursomes were halved. In the afternoon the Americans were put away smartly as the top four singles were all won by the home side, including Jody at number four in the order, where he beat Courville 3&2 to score the winning point. The weather for the day was dreadful, but no one cared. The final score was GB&I 14, USA 10 and Pádraig felt ready for the professional ranks.

Pádraig and Jody line up a putt on the 13th hole during the 1995 Walker Cup at Royal Porthcawl, Wales, which GB&I won 14–10.

CHAPTER TWO: 1995–2000

World in motion

Dermot Gilleece

Rich autumnal colours adorned The K Club for the inaugural staging of the Smurfit European Open in late September 1995. It was a lot like the way Oak Hill had looked the previous weekend in what was proving to be an extended Indian summer for Irish golf, embracing as it did a memorable contribution to the Walker Cup triumph at Royal Porthcawl on the ninth and tenth of the month, and the historic landing by Concorde at Dublin Airport on Monday the twenty-fifth. The country had never known anything quite like it. Further thrills were anticipated from Europe's returning Ryder Cup heroes, who included Dublin's own Philip Walton, scorer of the winning point against the USA at Oak Hill. With so much going on, it seemed like an ideal opportunity for an aspiring tournament professional to slip quietly into the paid ranks.

The early signs were decidedly good for Pádraig Harrington. A planned practice round on the Tuesday with long-time friend Paul McGinley was transformed into a surprisingly delightful experience when the pair found Bernhard Langer waiting for them on the first tee. The distinguished German golfer would go on to take the title after a play-off and would later become a hugely influential role model in Pádraig's tournament career. And as a bonus, the professional débutant had a clubhouse locker directly beside perennial Order of Merit winner Colin Montgomerie.

By Wednesday, however, the mood had changed. With deep concern etched into his earnest young face, Pádraig remarked ruefully, 'Well-wishers have been telling me that there's no difference in playing as a professional. Well, I've

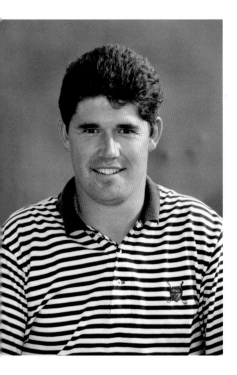

discovered one.' He had been stunned to learn that while his sixty-degree L-wedge was perfectly acceptable in amateur events, it was illegal on the European Tour at that time, because of its square grooves. And so it was that on the eve of the tournament, Pádraig began a desperate search for a club to replace one which he described as the third most important in his bag, after the driver and putter. 'I use it for everything from bunker play to chipping,' he said. (Little could he have imagined that twelve years later a similar implement would deliver the most crucial pitch of his career, in The Open Championship at Carnoustie.) Eventually, the problem was solved by Headfort professional Brendan McGovern, who generously supplied a replacement. (It is fascinating to note that he, too, was destined to play a critical role in Pádraig's Carnoustie triumph, albeit as a vanquished opponent a week earlier.)

A great adventure got under way in the company of Costantino Rocca and the eventual runner-up, Barry Lane. A measure of Pádraig's modest aspirations at the time was that he saw himself progressing ultimately to the status of no more than a journeyman pro. And what would it matter if he fell short of this target? There was always the safety net of his accountancy qualifications.

His brother Tadhg was on his bag that week, as he had been throughout Pádraig's amateur career. And there were no recriminations after rounds of 77 and 73 delivered a halfway total two strokes outside the cut. As he put it himself, 'I'm really thrilled to have been given this opportunity.' The ice had been broken, and far more meaningful challenges lay ahead in the form of two stages of the European Tour School, culminating on 23 to 28 November at San Roque and Guadalmina on Spain's Costa del Sol, where Tadhg would again be by his side.

Sixteenth place in the Qualifying School seemed a fair representation of Pádraig's aspirations. Though it confirmed the talent we had all become aware of during his amateur days, there was certainly nothing to indicate the dramatic events of a wonderful début season, then only a few months away. 'I have tried to learn from people,' he said at the time. 'If I feel there is something I need to know, I'll ask a person who can give me the answer. And I'll listen to what others tell me, even if I don't necessarily take their advice.'

This was the sort of thinking that led him to choose the grizzled bagman John O'Reilly from Tallaght as his first professional caddie for the 1996 season. The sceptics among us could see it only as a highly improbable partnership between an ageing rogue with a taste for cigarettes and a pint, and a clean-cut teetotaller and

non-smoker, who would have a newcomer's eye for
efficiency. But Pádraig saw things differently. He
saw a hugely experienced ally who had worked
with Peter Townsend and Des Smyth, and who
could guide a rookie safely through the maelstrom
of a tournament schedule spanning numerous
countries and time-zones. Events would prove it to
be an inspired decision. Indeed, one had only to
look at early results to see a productive partnership
in action. In his first eight events of the 1996
season, Pádraig finished 49th, 31st, 23rd, 45th,
48th, 8th, 7th and 10th. Then, after the Italian
Open, he headed for Madrid and the celebrated
terrain of Club de Campo.

For whatever reason, the Spanish capital
seems to hold a special appeal for Irish tournament
professionals. A quick scan through the results of
the Madrid Open reveals that Jimmy Kinsella was
victorious in 1972 and there were back-to-back
Irish successes from David Feherty and Des Smyth,
in 1992 and 1993. Never mind that these came at
Puerto de Hierro; the magic clearly emanated from
the ancient city.

There's also something about the world of golf
which often makes us think of it as no more than
a slightly overgrown village. The 1996 Spanish
Open at Club de Campo could be considered one
such instance, given that Pádraig was joined
among the newcomers in the field by a sixteen-
year-old amateur with a rapidly growing reputation.
The gifted Sergio Garcia from Castillon had the
distinction of carding an opening 68, which was
two strokes better than the rookie professional
from Dublin. Pádraig soon made his mark,
however, to sweep into a three-stroke lead with
a sparkling eight-under-par 64 on the Friday; he
needed only twenty-five putts, gripping the putter
right hand below for left-to-right breaking putts,
and left below right for those going the other way.

Pádraig celebrates the Spanish Open victory with his mum, Breda, and Caroline, who he marries less then two years later.

By that stage, delays due to electric storms were relatively short, but when the heavens opened in earnest on Saturday the third round had to be postponed. Then, after a decision had been taken to play thirty-six holes on the Sunday, rising temperatures caused the course to be shrouded in mist. So there was another delay, this time of two hours' duration.

It wasn't a situation likely to ease edgy, inexperienced nerves. But those locals who arrived on the Sunday morning wondering about this talented young Irishman had decided by lunchtime that they were witnessing a bright new talent on tour. On a course Seve Ballesteros claimed was playing longer than he had ever known it, Pádraig shot a third-round 67 to go six strokes clear of his closest challengers. When he birdied the opening hole of his final round in the afternoon, any lingering doubts were removed as to his ability to go all the way. With a closing 71 for a sixteen-under-par aggregate of 272, he claimed top prize of £91,660 by a four-stroke margin over second-placed Gordon Brand Jr. The crucial breakthrough had been achieved, considerably sooner than even his most optimistic admirers could have imagined. Garcia, meanwhile, did remarkably well for one so young, sharing forty-ninth place with Ballesteros (among others) on a one-over-par aggregate of 289.

Then Pádraig received a bitter lesson in the relentlessly demanding nature of tournament golf. It happened four days after Madrid, in the opening round of the Benson and Hedges International at The Oxfordshire. He changed the wet-gear of Spain for the woolly hat and sweater weather of mid-May in England as he prepared to play with Nick Faldo. In the most extreme contrast imaginable, Faldo shot a hole-in-one on the short 13th, and Pádraig took a wretched thirteen strokes to complete the long 17th. With the option of playing the hole around a lake as a 585-yard three-shotter or carrying the water with a long second, Pádraig elected to take on the carry. In a manner of speaking, he lost the election. Several times over. 'I didn't feel embarrassed because I tried on every shot,' he said afterwards in the media centre. 'The problem was that I know I can hit my three wood 250 yards downwind, but I forgot the first 240 yards were over water.' With the help of their golf correspondent John Hopkins, the following morning *The Times* produced a detailed graphic of Pádraig's play on that 17th hole. And our man's reaction? He cut out the graphic and placed it over the mantelpiece at home, as a stark reminder of what can go wrong on a golf course.

The learning process continued with a share of third place behind Marc Farry in the rain-restricted BMW International Open in Munich a few weeks later, and in a Dunhill Cup début in October. Then came another team appearance, in the World Cup, in which he partnered Darren Clarke for the event's first-ever South African staging, at Erinvale. That was where I first became aware of Pádraig Harrington, the masterly manager of time. Early in the week, as I sat in the clubhouse lounge, Pádraig approached me and enquired if I would need him for interview. Slightly taken aback, I informed him that, yes, I would. Whereupon he replied, 'Well, can we do it now, because I want to get in some practice.' In my experience it was a rare acknowledgement by a tournament professional that since both of us had a job to do perhaps we could help each other.

'For nine years as an amateur my main objective was to play representative golf,' Pádraig said, 'and the attraction has not diminished since I turned professional.' In those embryonic years he was, you may recall, beaten by Clarke in the semi-finals of the South of Ireland Championship in July 1990 and in the final of the Irish Close at Baltray a month later. 'I was totally in awe of Darren back then,' he acknowledged. 'He was a fantastic player, totally unbeatable in my view.' Now they were to be professional partners. It was a great disappointment that despite a fine closing 64 from Clarke, they finished no better than nineteenth behind the rampant home pair of Ernie Els and Wayne Westner. Clearly, the mental and emotional strain of a remarkable début season had taken its toll on Pádraig, especially in a final round of 78, which may have cost him an outside chance of taking the Rookie of the Year award ahead of Thomas Bjorn, who produced a considerably stronger World Cup performance.

But there was compensation down the line. Pádraig was accorded a unique distinction by the Irish Golf Writers' Association, who selected him as their Professional of the Year, twelve months after choosing him for the Leading Amateur award. In a memorable rookie season he had captured the Spanish Open, recorded a stroke average of 71.39 (tied twelfth) for twenty-eight tournaments and carded a total of 329 birdies, leaving him sixth in that particular category. And on the way to victory in Madrid, his lead of six strokes after fifty-four holes tied the best of the season with Tom Lehman (Open Championship) and Ian Woosnam (Volvo German Open).

Consolidation was the prime objective for 1997, when Pádraig would face the variety artiste's nightmare of appearing after the top act on a concert bill – only in this instance, the star performer he was attempting to emulate happened to be himself. By his own admission, 1996 had been 'phenomenal – beyond my wildest dreams'. Inevitably, public expectations of him had been raised. Apart from his obvious golfing skills, he was viewed as a remarkably stable young man who always seemed to make the right move, whether in terms of securing commercial deals or communicating with the media. He was confident without being brash; mannerly without being obsequious. There was talk of a Ryder Cup début at Valderrama in September of that year, though at nineteenth in the team standings at the Christmas break he considered himself to be way out of contention. 'I haven't a clue how I'll come out of the blocks this time,' he admitted. 'But I'm going to give myself time to settle in. This time last year, I managed to play in only one of the first six tournaments. Now, I have the freedom to play all six.' Which is what he did, making the cut in all of them, starting with the Johnnie Walker Classic at Hope Island, on his first trip to Australia.

Typically methodical, Pádraig wrote down twelve targets for the season, and among those he was prepared to divulge were to end 1997 in the top fifty of the Order of Merit; to make as many cuts (twenty) as he did in 1996; and that one of those cuts would be in his first US Open, at Congressional. He also wanted to retain his place on the Ireland team for the Alfred Dunhill Cup and the World Cup. And he had convinced himself that finishing runner-up wasn't necessarily a bad thing. 'Handling that level of disappointment has helped me become a more mature person,' he said. 'And I've got to try and shut myself off from the expectations of others, however well intentioned they may be.' Behind the pragmatism, however, there was an obvious delight in the life his talent and application had opened up for him. And there was an awareness that the achievements of his rookie season had permitted him the luxury of striving to become a better player, rather than being consigned to a battle for survival. As he put it, 'I'm in this for the long haul.' All of which was music to the ears of his caddie, John O'Reilly, who enjoyed nothing better than working out his percentage of his master's winnings.

There was no reward at Congressional, where severe dehydration greatly reduced his prospects of making the cut, but Pádraig surpassed his own

John O'Reilly was on Pádraig's bag from the start of the 1996 season, witnessing many early successes.

On top of the world –
Paul McGinley and
Pádraig win the World
Cup for Ireland, the first
time in thirty-nine years,
at the Ocean Course,
Kiawah Island, USA.

expectations in The Open Championship at Royal Troon. From tied seventeenth on Saturday night, he swept up the order with each passing hole of a dramatic final round. Ultimately, a brilliant four-under-par 67 for an aggregate of 280 earned him a share of fifth place behind Justin Leonard for £62,500. Typically, he didn't want to talk about money afterwards. 'I can only think how tremendous it is for me to finish in the top ten of a major championship,' he said. 'My main objective was to get into the top fifteen for an exemption for next year's event, so I've every reason to be happy.' Still, it was a handsome cheque. Small wonder that he also remarked, 'In terms of importance, this ranks pretty close to the Spanish Open win.'

The performance at Troon meant he retained his place as Clarke's partner in the Irish team for the World Cup in Kiawah Island in November. When Clarke decided to opt out, Ireland had a new partnership of old friends, Paul McGinley making it a Dublin duo.

A moderately fertile imagination could have concluded that John O'Reilly's contribution to the Irish effort at Kiawah Island was defined by events in the Dunhill Cup a month earlier. After Irish defeats at the hands of South Africa and Scotland, the caddie received disproportionate attention from Sky commentator Ewen Murray, who, on seeing 'Irish John' limping, suggested it was the result of a mosquito bite. And that the unfortunate bug had been whisked off to the Betty Ford Clinic for treatment. Pádraig loved that story, and how O'Reilly had feigned deep hurt, even to the point of threatening to sue, after the ribbing he got from his pals in Tallaght. 'Joining in the fun, John agreed to back off if the TV commentators would announce that the mosquito had since been totally rehabilitated and released from the clinic,' he recalled. 'And as for being fond of a jar, John pointed out that one of the commentators was known as Lebanon, he was bombed so often.'

Apart from carrying out his normal caddying duties at Kiawah, O'Reilly would have to ensure that neither Irish player fell victim to boredom during a notoriously slow event. As Pádraig remarked, 'Whatever you say about previous years, we were fully prepared for six-hour rounds at Kiawah. In that respect, part of John's job was to help us all with his good-spirited chat, keeping us entertained.' And clearly he did superbly on that front: the Irish duo captured the title by six strokes from second-placed Scotland, with the formidable US pairing of Davis Love and Open champion Leonard third. Later, Pádraig said, 'On a one to one, I find John very entertaining. And he's extremely obliging – a man who loves doing favours for people. And from a caddying standpoint, he has tremendous experience from his twenty-four years on the tour, with an instinctive feeling for the right club to use, without reference to distance.'

Like most people, Pádraig had first heard of Kiawah Island when the Ryder Cup was staged there in 1991. He remembered playing in the Carlow Scratch Cup that weekend, and tuning into the radio commentary as he drove home on the Sunday evening. He got into the house just in time to see Bernhard Langer on the last hole, missing that infamous six-foot putt. Little could he have imagined that he would face a similar par-putt himself, in the second round of the World Cup, six years later. 'Standing over the ball, I realized it was exactly the putt Langer had missed,' he recalled. Unlike the hapless German, he holed it.

After three holes at Kiawah on Sunday, Ireland took the lead for the first time. By the ninth, the Scots had dropped totally out of contention. Only then did Pádraig allow himself to think that he and Paul were in a position to win.

Frequently, one could see the shadow of a smile flicker across their faces, as if they were sharing a private joke. And all the while there was a clear emphasis on playing one's own game. Afterwards, McGinley claimed, 'I felt fairly comfortable throughout.' But his partner admitted, sheepishly, 'I was trying my best to look comfortable.'

Their victory bridged a thirty-nine-year gap back to 1958 and Harry Bradshaw and Christy O'Connor Sr, who captured what was then the Canada Cup for Ireland. And it seemed to strengthen the bond between players who had been close friends and golfing colleagues since their teen years in Rathfarnham. They had become Walker Cup partners after being unbeaten in foursomes for Ireland during the European Amateur Team Championship in Madrid in 1991. Significantly, that was Pádraig's first experience of Club de Campo, and he loved it, taking a maximum six points from six matches. Pádraig knew about Himself and the Brad; he also knew that such legendary figures as Jack Nicklaus, Johnny Miller, Arnold Palmer, Ben Hogan and Sam Snead were on the tournament's roll of honour. 'No wonder our win has meant so much to everybody,' he remarked. A lasting memory for me of the victory scenes was of O'Reilly being handed a wad of dollars by Pádraig to buy drinks for the many well-wishers. And with that mischievous, gummy grin of his, it seemed to me the caddie had never looked happier.

The players' decision to stay overnight allowed them to savour the local reaction to their magnificent triumph. They received the full treatment on the front page of Charleston's *Post and Courier* the next morning, where they were photographed holding the trophy under the headline 'On Top of the World'.

Later, at Stackstown, where I was interviewing Pádraig for an end-of-year piece, I remember being somewhat taken aback when he drove up to the club in a modest Honda Civic. Here was a player on top of the golfing world who seemed to have no difficulty in keeping his feet firmly on the ground. He even had the good sense to marry his long-time girlfriend Caroline shortly afterwards, on 6 December.

By comparison with Pádraig's first two years on tour, 1998 was marked by relatively modest achievement. Granted, there was a win in the Irish Professional Championship at Powerscourt, and he made his first cut in a US Open. With only two three-putts over the four rounds he was tied thirty-second behind Lee Janzen at the Olympic Club after a thirteen-over-par aggregate of 293.

He gained most satisfaction, however, from starting work in late summer with coach Bob Torrance. While acknowledging that he had got greater height into his shots at the Olympic Club, Pádraig knew he was only scratching the surface in terms of where he wanted his game to be. And he was convinced that the gravel-voiced, chain-smoking Scot could take him there. Certainly a world ranking of 107th at the end of November 1998 was not acceptable.

After he and McGinley had made a spirited defence of the World Cup with a sixth-place finish in Auckland, Pádraig took seven weeks off. 'I really needed that, to relax and enjoy life,' he said early in 1999. 'Actually it would have been a more extended break if I'd a bit more confidence in my game.' He also joined a gym to improve his fitness, and lost about a stone in weight. And with the New Year still in its infancy, he had already flown twice to Scotland for sessions with Torrance at his home in Largs. 'Though I'm mentally stronger, my total of tournaments (in 1999) will be twenty-eight compared with thirty-six in my first year,' he said. 'Having looked at how I prepared as an amateur, I've concluded that I perform better when I take time away from the game. Over the last two years, I hardly took a day off except for travelling. Now, every time I play a tournament I'm going to have two days' rest, at least.' (Of course, he never did.)

As husband and wife, he and Caroline were very much a modern couple, travelling the world together and sharing the highs and lows of tournament life. I vividly recall her during the 1999 World Cup in Kuala Lumpur, flinging a sandwich to her husband as he stepped off the 10th tee. Later, she asked if I would mind her sitting beside me in the media centre while she took details from the scoreboard for Pádraig's benefit. As for the player himself, a remarkable equanimity made him a welcome partner on the golf course, and invariably a responsive, helpful interviewee off it.

To borrow a line from a much-loved Frank Sinatra ballad, 1999 was a very good year. There was a splendid Ryder Cup début at Brookline,

Pádraig relaxes during a rain delay at the 1998 Italian Open.

five second places, a couple of fourth places and a sixth place – and qualification for a US Masters début in 2000, courtesy of making the world's top fifty. The accumulation of second-place finishes, however, was becoming a matter of some concern. As Pádraig acknowledged, 'It's a pity to have lost so many tournaments. I certainly saw the Italian Open and German Masters as losses. Though I finished with a 67 in Germany, I still bogeyed the last. And I should have done better than a final-round 70 in Italy.' On the plus side, however, the high draw he had developed as a result of working with Torrance had lengthened his drives from 255 to 280 yards. Yet he insisted impatiently, 'Maybe I am better than I was, but all I can see are the things I want to improve. In my way, I realize I'm looking for perfection, but that's the way I am.'

Still, the rewards continued to flow. Few experiences could have been better than the São Paulo 500 Years Open in early April 2000, where his second European Tour victory arrived courtesy of a two-stroke margin over American

Gerry Norquist. The win lifted him to a highest-ever thirty-seventh in the world rankings. Having felt rusty after missing the cut at Bay Hill on St Patrick's Day, Pádraig had thought of Brazil and the Rio de Janeiro 500 Years Open, scheduled for 23 to 26 March. 'Entries closed at midday on the Saturday and I sought a sponsor's invitation at nine the previous night,' he said. 'It must rank as one of the best decisions of my professional career so far.' As it happened, he was second to Roger Chapman in Rio, before going on to victory the following week in São Paulo.

At lunchtime the day after he captured that title in Brazil, as his driver headed into Magnolia Lane Pádraig memorably turned to Caroline and whispered, 'Shhh. We're here.' After that, the Masters débutant began to absorb every detail of a place he had seen only on television, a place that was a world away from the teeming city of São Paulo. It was everything he had imagined, and within minutes he was listening to the legendary Sam Snead holding court on the clubhouse veranda. Later, as only the seventh Irishman ever to compete in the Masters, he did himself proud with a share of nineteenth place behind Vijay Singh. Indeed, with the experienced Dave McNeilly now on his bag, he'd actually claimed a share of the clubhouse lead on 291 after a two-putt par on the 72nd. His verdict? 'I have never had such a testing golfing experience. I hope to be coming back here again and again to learn all the new things there are to be learned about this wonderful course. After all, Bernhard Langer has been coming here eighteen years and he tells me he's still learning.'

Then, in the almost inevitable way of golf, a thrilling high was followed by a crushing low, little more than a month later. It happened in the Benson and Hedges International at The Belfry. As the result of a devastating mix-up involving playing partner Jamie Spence, it was discovered an hour before he was due to set off on his final round on the Sunday as the leader by five strokes that Pádraig had failed to sign for an opening 71. When the error was brought to his attention, he accepted the disqualification with such dignity as to prompt glowing tributes, even at the highest level of the

Pádraig's first Masters appearance in 2000 saw him finish in the top twenty and vow to return. He is pictured here putting during the second round.

Hole	1	2	3	4	5	6	7	8	9	Out
Metres	376	347	492	404	373	361	162	391	396	3302
Yards	411	379	538	442	408	395	177	426	433	3611
Par	4	4	5	4	4	4	3	4	4	36
Score	6	5	5	4	4	4	2	4	4	38

Match: 31 Time: 12.55
Date: 11 MAY 00
Padraig HARRINGTON (Ire)
Round: 1
Tee: 1

**BENSON and HEDGES
INTERNATIONAL OPEN
2000**
THE BRABAZON COURSE, THE BELFRY
Thursday 11th – Sunday 14th May 2000

Hole	10	11	12	13	14	15	16	17	18	In	Total
Metres	284	383	190	351	174	498	378	516	433	3207	6509
Yards	311	419	208	384	190	544	413	564	473	3502	7118
Par	4	4	3	4	3	5	4	5	4	36	72
Score	3	5	3	4	2	4	4	5	3	33	71

Signature of Marker

Signature of Competitor

A score of 71 in the first round of the 2000 Benson and Hedges International was subsequently ruled out as the scorecard was found not to include Pádraig's signature.

game. 'We've talked about the matter here and I don't think it would be inaccurate to say that everybody was incredibly impressed,' said Grant Moir of the Rules of Golf committee of the R&A. 'I don't think he can be praised highly enough for the way he handled what must have been a very difficult situation. He has come out of it with great credit. It was particularly admirable that he did not attempt to ascribe blame to anybody else; that it is something [countersigning his scorecard] he had been doing since he was twelve years old and he knew the rules. It's always nice to see a professional react in that way. Through his conduct, he has won himself more admirers than he could ever have done through winning a golf competition.'

Four weeks later, in the build-up to the US Open at Pebble Beach, we got some insight into the price Pádraig had to pay for the trauma of those events. 'I lost three kilos [about six and a half pounds] in weight in the aftermath of The Belfry, but I've since put it back on,' he said. 'That's what stress does to you. The experience was obviously eating into me and I didn't know it. And it wasn't as if I was shedding superfluous weight: it was muscle loss.'

As with Augusta National two months earlier, he was captivated by his first sight of another famous venue. 'It's visually breathtaking, better than anything I had imagined,' he said. 'And I really like the course.' Any notion that he might have become heartily sick of paying his dues to a notoriously demanding game was emphatically removed late on the Friday evening. The last stroke he executed before play was suspended in the second round was a ten-foot putt on the 9th, just after the ball had moved backwards into a depression. 'Nobody saw it except me,' he said. 'What bothers me is that these things come in threes and I'm wondering

when the third one is going to happen.' In the event, he duly called a one-stroke penalty on himself and then sank the ten-footer for a bogey, en route to a 71. Despite the extraordinary dominance of Tiger Woods, who captured the title by fifteen strokes, it was a richly rewarding championship for Pádraig. With an aggregate of 289, he was tied fifth, thus becoming the highest-placed Irishman in the history of the championship, surpassing the share of seventh place by Greenore's Peter O'Hare at Oakland Hills in 1924.

July brought a tied twentieth finish in The Open Championship at St Andrews, and a month later he was tied fifty-eighth in the US PGA Championship at Valhalla. It meant he had gained the distinction of making the cut in the four majors in his first year of playing them all. And the season wasn't over yet.

Despite calling a penalty shot upon himself, Pádraig finished in fifth place at the 2000 US Open at Pebble Beach.

Below Pádraig plays his approach shot to the 18th hole in the final round of the 2000 Turespaña Masters at Club de Campo, Madrid.

Opposite Pádraig salutes the crowd after holing out on the last hole to claim the Turespaña Masters title, helping him to finish seventh on the final European Tour Order of Merit.

With a second tournament win of the season, Pádraig moved up another significant rung on the ladder towards world prominence. As with Rio de Janeiro, his entry for the Turespaña Masters in Madrid at the end of October was a late decision. And his thinking was greatly influenced by the fact that the tournament was at Club de Campo. En route to a two-stroke victory over Gary Orr, he carded a second-round 64, just as he had done when capturing the Spanish Open on the same course in 1996. And good memories became a priceless asset after a potentially disastrous double-bogey six at the 13th in his final round. That was when he reminded himself of how he had handled the run-in four years earlier. The ship was steadied and a hugely important victory was secured, in the context of events at The Belfry five months earlier. It also lent a fascinating dimension to Pádraig's claim that he needed to be pressurized in order to concentrate properly – such as when he battled with severe neck and shoulder pain at Firestone earlier that year and declared that his target was 'not to finish last'.

Out of such quiet determination, a sparkling career was about to blossom.

CHAPTER THREE: 2001–2005
Rise and shine

Karl MacGinty

It's like mounting an expedition to your personal Everest. At the outset you can see the high peaks in the distance. They're beautiful but remote, almost irrelevant as you take your first steps on the rising road into the foothills. Some keep their eye to the path as they travel, but Pádraig Harrington never lost sight of the summit, working tirelessly on those early slopes and endlessly girding himself for the peaks and valleys that lay ahead.

The Dubliner never took the easy path as he pressed onwards, ever upwards. And in caddie Dave McNeilly and gnarled Scottish coach Bob Torrance he had found men as passionate, hard-working and hungry as himself. Dr Bob Rotella would never cease advising him that 'Golf Is Not a Game of Perfect', but Pádraig and 'Sherpa' Dave relentlessly sought perfection none the less, burning out the light bulbs on practice ranges all around the world – like Ben Hogan, 'digging it out of the dirt'.

In 2001, Pádraig began to notice that the slopes were getting ever steeper and the air was growing thin. Suddenly he found himself climbing in more exalted company, scaling the world rankings at a pace which occasionally surprised even him. He was entering a new level in the game. Much would happen over the next four years to advance the process of moulding him into the man and the champion he has become. In his personal life during this time he would

Pádraig misses a birdie putt on the second extra hole in the play-off with Vijay Singh at Saujana Golf and Country Club, Kuala Lumpur during the 2001 Malaysian Open.

be blessed by the birth of his first child, Patrick, in 2003; and he would mourn the loss two years later of his beloved father. On the golf course he would learn priceless lessons about himself through mould-breaking triumphs in Europe and then the United States, plus a litany of second places, not all of which can truly be dismissed as defeats.

After beginning 2001 in twenty-first place in the world rankings, Pádraig found himself at fourteen by mid-July, ahead of household names such as Nick Price and recently crowned US Open champion Retief Goosen. Come November, his victory in the Volvo Masters propelled him into the world's top ten. On both occasions he paused on golf's rock face to look down . . . and felt dizzy. Utterly engrossed in his hand-by-foot ascent, the Dubliner was surprised, even intimidated, by how high he'd climbed. 'I remember when I got to number fourteen in the world, it really hit me hard,' he says. 'I thought to myself, "Hold on a minute, am I really the fourteenth best player in the world? Look at all those people I'd have put on a pedestal, and now I'm in there with them. Nah, this can't be right." I had the exact same feeling when I got into the top ten. It was only when I drifted out and came back in again that I felt comfortable there; but the first time it was a very strange feeling. This has always been the case with me. I nearly have to double-do something before I can really do it. I have to get so close that I convince myself I'm good enough to win something before I actually believe in my head "I can do this". There's a level of uncertainty I always have to breach.'

This nagging sense that he needed to run just to keep up fuelled Pádraig's fearsome work ethic in his formative years as a professional. Yet as he eased into the upper echelons of the game, it began to work against him as exhaustive and exhausting hours on the range during tournaments took their toll on too many Sunday afternoons. He finished second six times on the European Tour in 2001, including a play-off defeat against reigning US Masters champion Vijay Singh at the Malaysian Open, Pádraig's first event of the year.

The tropical heat of Kuala Lumpur was the perfect opportunity for Pádraig to warm muscles and joints stiffened by the Irish winter. He happens to like the golf course at Saujana, despite the occasional run-in with mischievous little monkeys who like to open the zips of golf bags and pinch anything they find inside. I remember arriving once in the Malaysian capital exhausted after a sleepless thirty-two-hour *Planes, Trains and Automobiles*-style trip from Ireland, and utterly stuck for a story for the next day's paper. Then I bumped into Pádraig in the restaurant at Saujana. 'Look,' he said in exasperation, proffering me his laser range-finder, which was chipped, cracked and riddled with little tooth marks. 'A monkey stole it out of my bag and ran up a tree with it. A local caddie went up the tree to get it back, but not before the monkey bit lumps out of it.' The story of Pádraig Harrington's run-in with Saujana's monkeys went all around the world.

However, in 2001 it wasn't destruction of their equipment that stirred Pádraig's caddie, Dave McNeilly, into a rage. He gave a real dressing down to Vijay Singh after the player drove through Harrington's group in practice as the Irishman putted out on the dog-legged par-four 17th. McNeilly's one of the nicest chaps you'd ever hope to meet, but once that red mist descends, he has that glorious Irish trait of being able to wield words like meat cleavers.

Hole 17 would have a significant bearing on the outcome of the tournament. For a start, Singh, playing in the group ahead of Pádraig in the final round, shot a double-bogey there to fall two strokes off the pace being set by Pádraig after birdies at 15 and 16. Then the strident quack of a duck or some other waterfowl clipped Pádraig's wings at 17. 'I was standing over my ball in mid-fairway when a swan or a duck started to act up just as I was about to hit my shot,' he explains. 'So I backed off the shot, didn't go through my usual routine, and instead of hitting a smooth lob wedge I hit a firmish one and it went over the green for bogey.' After Singh birdied the last to tie with Pádraig, the Dubliner shaved the hole with his own fifteen-footer for outright victory. Still deadlocked after two trips up 18 in the play-off, they headed next to 17, where the two Irishmen firmly believed a wrong would be righted in their favour. 'When Dave and I got to seventeen in the play-off, we were both convinced fate was at work. That we'd win out at that hole and justice would be served. Sadly, we were wrong. Vijay and I both hit a driver. Mine went on to the bank on the right edge of the green, while Vijay's went through the back. I didn't chip it up the tier on the green and missed the putt, while Vijay made his putt and that was the end of that. He'd won it, fair and square. That's the way it goes. Obviously in the last year [2006/07] things have worked out for me. I've won four play-offs, so, in a strange way, everything seems to balance out in golf . . . and that's how I regard all those second places as well.'

Whether it's a lesson learned, a milestone passed or a millstone shed, Pádraig Harrington seems to take something from every tournament he plays. He left Kuala Lumpur that Sunday with one mantra ringing in his head. Identifying that simple mental error on the fairway at 17 in regulation on Sunday as the difference between victory and defeat, he insists, 'The mistake was breaking my routine and not getting fully back into it. Distractions aren't the problem; it's how you recover from them that's important.'

A fortnight later, Pádraig hit the proverbial wall late on Sunday in Dubai. Buoyed by a splendid 64 on Saturday, he actually took the lead into the back nine on his final round before bogeys at 12 and 15 sent him tumbling back into an anonymous tie for second place with Tiger Woods behind a truly spectacular winner, Thomas Bjorn. 'I might as well not have been in the event,' he said. 'I think I might have been four or five under par for the first nine holes and just hit a wall. That was it. I needed another three under par on the back nine and couldn't get it. I think I actually ran out of steam. I had just done too much work in the week. At every tournament I played, I'd practise until half six or seven each day. But they've floodlights in Dubai and I remember they had to kick me off the range every night at eight o'clock. I definitely led the European statistics for closing driving ranges. I cannot count the number of times Dave went out to gather balls from the range after we'd been refused one last bucket. I'd keep hitting them out as he brought them back in.'

Pádraig has absolutely no regrets about the time and energy he invested in perfecting his swing, but it was costing money. 'When I first came out on Tour in

Pádraig and Vijay Singh stride down the 17th hole to play the third extra hole at Saujana during the play-off, which Vijay won with a birdie.

1996, I kept my head down and did my thing. Yes, I practised, but everything was about getting my game ready to play each week. It was one tournament at a time. Then, in 1998, I started changing my game with Bob Torrance. Through the next few years there was a lot of hard work and everything was about my swing. Though I kept working on my game from 2001 to 2005, the balance between practice and play began to shift. I was developing as a golfer. I was out there trying to win tournaments. I can remember so many times during that period when I had genuine chances to win tournaments but I definitely made a lot of mistakes. Looking back now, I know where it probably went wrong – not on the course but in the amount of work I was doing when everything really was OK with my game. If you are in contention on the Saturday at a tournament, you're obviously playing good golf. Why, then, would you need to go out and spend three hours working on your swing on a Saturday evening? When I should have been getting my head ready for the next day, I was getting my swing ready.'

Every one of Pádraig's second places has a story. He played well in the Algarve in 2001, but by his own admission he couldn't buy a putt as he posted 70 in the final round and lost out only to a brilliant 64 by Philip Price. 'That was annoying. To play so well and not win baffled me a bit. It confused me. Why me? How could I play so well and lose? How unlucky am I? Now I realize that much of it was down to mental sharpness, just getting my head in the right place.'

Pádraig posted a 64 himself in the final round of that year's Murphy's Irish Open at Fota but had no chance of catching the imperious Colin Montgomerie. The following Sunday, Darren Clarke led the rest a merry dance at The K Club, finishing three ahead of Pádraig, Thomas Bjorn and Ian Woosnam, all of whom tied for second place.

No disgrace there, nor at the BMW International, where Pádraig was pipped by one stroke after rounds of 69, 63, 62 and 68 for a twenty-six-under-par total that John Daly beat by one as he claimed his first win since the 1995 Open. Daly's score would have tied the lowest aggregate in European Tour history had preferred lies not been granted in Saturday's third round, but Pádraig can be forgiven for not joining the outpourings of joy for the immensely popular American. 'You wouldn't believe how many people came up to me and said, "Isn't it great that John Daly's back?" Frankly, I was thinking, "Could he not have won the tournament the following week?" I'd played phenomenal golf, probably my best ever. I did hit it in the water at the last but still made par there. There definitely was another little bit of "What do I have to do to win one?" Portugal was like that too. In Malaysia we thought it was our destiny to win, but I was beaten fair and square. Dubai, I wasn't quite up to it, while I simply wasn't there at the Irish and European Opens. But the BMW really was a case of "Why me?"

'The most significant thing was that all through that year I shot incredibly low numbers. I was shooting 63s and 64s, scoring twenty under par and suchlike. I'm such a different player now. I'm more conservative. Back then I was forever firing at pins and seeking perfection all the time. These days I shoot 68 to 72 most of the time, though I wouldn't mind throwing in 62s or 63s a little more often.'

It must have been tiresome through 2001 for Pádraig to explain each second place to an increasingly intrigued public. 'It was the same rhetoric,' he explained. '"It's all OK, guys, I'm getting better, I'm improving." I believed it, but I needed some sort of proof for everyone else.' Irrefutable proof was provided in the Volvo Masters at Montecastillo, as Harrington brought his season in Europe to a stirring climax with the most significant of his four victories to that point on the Tour's international schedule, ironically denying fellow Dubliner and good friend Paul McGinley in the process.

The Volvo Masters was played for the fifth and final time that year in Jerez since being displaced from Valderrama by the 1997 Ryder Cup. Montecastillo's location next door to the international motor racing circuit appealed to Volvo, and Pádraig certainly wasn't objecting. As a golf course, it suited him a lot more than

Below Despite shooting 26 under par, Pádraig finished second to John Daly at the 2001 BMW International.

Opposite Pádraig punches the air as he holes his birdie putt on the 72nd hole of the 2001 Volvo Masters, beating close friend Paul McGinley by one shot at Montecastillo Golf Resort, Jerez to finish second on the final Order of Merit.

Valderrama, where he feels as comfortable as a man in an overcoat that's too tight. 'Montecastillo suited me,' confirms Pádraig, who finished second in the Volvo Masters there in 1997 and was runner-up once again in 1999. 'It's a big golf course and I make lots of birdies on it. I was never capable of going that low at Valderrama. It's tight and eats me up. There's not enough of getting the driver out, giving it a hit and going to find it. I play with much more flair on courses like that. When I get into trouble, I like to recover, but Valderrama gives you very little chance to do so.'

Interestingly, the howling gales that forced the third round of the 2001 Volvo Masters to be abandoned left the entire field, including Pádraig, with their feet up on Saturday. The Irishman had little option but to take it easy and sharpen his focus for Sunday, and judging by his exemplary performance over the closing six holes the following day, it made all the difference. 'I'd a good finish there,' he says. 'I played the last couple of holes well. I think I might have been four or five under for the last six or seven holes. It was one of those things. I kind of got into position at the right time and literally ran out of holes.'

For all of Pádraig's joy as his aggressive thirty-foot birdie putt on the final green dived into the cup, it was agony for McGinley, at that moment standing on the elevated 18th tee and watching his prospects of victory disappear down that hole with his fellow Irishman's ball. 'I'll never forget the absolute joy of holing that putt and the excitement of winning,' says Pádraig. 'That win was huge for me so it really was a punch-the-air moment. It's one of the few pictures I have up on the wall at home. Yet the absolute exhilaration I felt at that moment was tainted by the fact that I'd just beaten Paul. I've just won, and I'm so happy I want to shout it to the world, yet I've just beaten a

friend who needed that win just as much as I did. It really brought it home to me that I easily could have been in Paul's shoes that day and would have had to sit down and talk about yet another second place. Paul must have been thinking "Why me?" that Sunday.

'I've hit many good putts from thirty feet that haven't gone in. But it was a right-to-left putt and I was in the mindset of holing it. That's what happens. If the cameras were on my eyes that day, you'd have seen that they were wide open, ready to go. I had that look which I seem to get every so often. I just holed putts to beat the band. The [2007] Open was the same. When I get into that frame of mind I feel I can do incredible things. It could have gone by the hole and, who knows, I might have missed the one back. But it was my day and it was huge in the context of all that had happened [that year]. What it said to me was, "Hang around the right places and you will get your share; it will happen." All that year I'd been doing the right things but not getting the break at the right time, but I ended the year believing that good things do indeed happen to me.'

Pádraig ambled into 2002 with an even jauntier swing in his step, and his sights set on broader horizons. He now travelled in expectation rather than hope.

After making America's cognoscenti sit up and take note with his fifth place behind a rampant Tiger in the US Open at Pebble Beach in 2000, Pádraig justified his new status by finishing in the same spot behind the same man at the 2002 US Masters. And at the US Open that June in the beautiful bedlam of Bethpage State Park, Pádraig delighted the raucous New York Irish by emerging from a Friday maelstrom with an astonishing 68 to claim pride of place with Tiger in the final group on Saturday. This really was the big time. As Woods and Harrington strode on to the massive elevated first tee at Bethpage, they were greeted with a roar that would have done justice to Yankee Stadium or the Shea.

Though he revelled in the atmosphere and appeared to outsiders to be on the brink of

Pádraig reacts to a missed birdie putt on the 2nd hole during the second round of the 2002 Masters, where he finished fifth.

something really big, in his own heart Pádraig knew he wasn't ready to win a major. Everyone dreams, but Pádraig's sporting ambitions have always been based on hard work and cold reality. Seve Ballesteros, who broke the yoke for an entire generation of European golfers at the majors, insists you have to be able to see yourself donning the green jacket or lifting the Claret Jug if you are going to win it. You must believe! 'I didn't believe I had the ability to win the Masters that year, or the US Open,' admits the man whose faith was still invested in the pursuit of perfection. 'I just wasn't ready for it. I had won the big event in Europe but there was still more to be done. I didn't believe I was the finished article.'

Despite finishing eighth at the 2002 US Open on the Black Course at Bethpage, New York, Pádraig realized more work had to be done before he could win a major.

65

In truth, Pádraig didn't play well in 'Tiger World' that Saturday at Bethpage, posting a three-over-par 73 as the true darling of the New York crowd that week, Phil Mickelson, and their whipping boy, Sergio Garcia, thrust themselves into the role of 'Great Pretenders'. 'The atmosphere was phenomenal, probably the best I have seen at an individual event,' Pádraig recalls. 'I really loved Bethpage and had a great time. I was doing my own thing, but deep down I knew I had a lot to learn, and getting into the last group with Tiger on the weekend at a big, hyped-up tournament was part of that. You've got to do that again and again. When you are playing with Tiger in a situation like that, there are seventy cameramen down the side of the fairway and you have to wait for them to settle into their positions before you can play your shot. When you're not used to it, it's difficult, but I know about it now so it's not a problem. Back then I wasn't prepared for it. There's a few little things like that, but it's all part of the learning process. I walked away from Bethpage that Saturday thinking, "That's different." But it was a great experience. You have to go out there and do it.'

Pádraig went out there and very nearly did it the following month at Muirfield, getting within one stroke of the play-off for The Open Championship after delivering what he still insists were the best seventy-two holes of his life. 'That week was an anomaly,' he says. 'I would say it's the biggest blip in my whole career. It's what I am trying to be right now. I just went there and played the tournament for the tournament. I got right into the zone from the very start. It was unbelievable. I didn't let myself create that in any other tournament up until now. Though I putted like a womble that week, unbelievably poor, Muirfield is the best I've ever played by a long way, the best I've ever been for four rounds of golf, and it's been hard for me to re-create. It took me three days at Carnoustie [in 2007] to get into that zone. Compared to what I'm normally like, it was incredible how I played that week at Muirfield. It really told me something. It showed me my true potential.' Muirfield came out of the blue, though, so Pádraig remained convinced that he had a lot of work to do before he reached major championship-winning form. 'In the back of my mind I knew that was the standard I wanted to achieve, though there were many other things I wanted to do first before I'd allow myself to get there.' Performance-wise, it wasn't Everest, more like Annapurna.

Yet the public in Ireland, already stunned by their hero's failure to apply the coup de grâce to Michael Campbell on the final hole of the European Open at The K Club two Sundays earlier, fixated on the Dubliner's wayward final tee shot at Muirfield. For the first time that week, Pádraig had taken out the driver at 18 and pulled his ball into the face of a fairway bunker, leaving him with no option but to play his second out sideways and into a public viewing area. 'The last hole is a tough par four but I was two or three shots behind and, looking back, there was no

way anyone would have predicted the scores that got into the play-off. I played
the last six holes in about three under and Ernie [Els] played them in three over,
so there was no way of knowing what was going to happen. Dave told me the
situation as we stood on the tee, and after discussing what club to hit it was "Yeah,
let's go for it, let's take it on. We'll hit the shots and play the hole for birdie."
I haven't putted well, so to make that birdie I think I have to hit driver, then
nine iron into that back pin. Because of where it was, it was easier to get to with
a spinning approach shot. If I lay back off the tee, it's a long shot [to the green],
I end up making par and I finish second. People would say, "Ah well, good
performance." As far as I was concerned, hitting that driver would at least give me
a chance of winning the tournament. Stuart Appleby did the exact opposite to me.
He played an iron off the tee, and Dave and I stood there wondering, "Why is this
guy playing for second place?" As it happened, he hit another long iron on to the
green and made the putt for birdie to get into the play-off.

'I hit a bad drive, like I did at the eighteenth hole at Carnoustie [in 2007],' he
confesses. 'It was the exact same swing. One went right, the other left, but there

Pádraig plays from the
first tee in the final round
of the 2002 Open
Championship at
Muirfield, Scotland.
A hooked drive into a
bunker on the 72nd hole,
resulting in a bogey,
meant that Pádraig
missed out on a play-off
by one shot.

wasn't a hell of a lot of difference between the two of them. My routine broke down. There was trouble out there at 330 yards on the right-hand side of the eighteenth fairway at Muirfield, the heaviest piece of rough I'd probably seen on the golf course. If I hit it in there, I wasn't going to be doing anything with my golf ball. Another player probably wouldn't have been aware of that little area, about ten yards wide. In my head, I told myself to avoid it, so that's exactly what I did. It's like I always say: be careful what you wish for. That's what I mean when I talk about focus. I chose the wrong thought on the tee. But I don't regret hitting a driver, I really don't. I was so disappointed afterwards, but looking at all the information at my disposal, I tried to play the right shot the right way. If I went back there tomorrow, I'd do the same again. Definitely!'

If Muirfield brought Pádraig Harrington close to perfection and let him know that somewhere inside he did indeed have the mental resilience to scale the game's highest peaks, a timely play-off win over Eduardo Romero at the Dunhill Links

Pictured at the Old Course, St Andrews, a play-off win in the 2002 Dunhill Links Championship thrust Pádraig into contention for the Order of Merit title.

Championship that October provided him with his biggest cheque to date – €818,662. Just as significantly, it thrust Pádraig into an end-of-season showdown with Retief Goosen at the top of the European Tour's Order of Merit. With around €40,000 separating them, their challenge became so tense and, out of the blue, Goosen made comments at a pre-tournament press conference at the Madrid Open, saying that the Dubliner was 'definitely the slowest player on Tour'. Pádraig, who used to have a reputation for slow play but had worked hard to remedy it, was able to accuse 'the kettle of calling the pot black' when Goosen himself fell behind schedule in Madrid and picked up 'a bad time' from a tournament referee. Suffice to say the two guys remain friends.

After playing with each other in the first round of the 2002 Volvo Masters at Valderrama, Retief Goosen narrowly clinched the Order of Merit title over Pádraig by less than €16,000.

Their race went right down to the wire at the Volvo Masters, where neither man cloaked himself in glory, Goosen winning the Order of Merit for the second year in succession by a paltry €15,573 after finishing in a tie for thirty-fourth at Valderrama, two places ahead of Pádraig.

Though Pádraig returned home from the Costa empty-handed that weekend, he had learned another priceless lesson. 'It's one of the textbook tournaments in my career,' he confirms. 'It showed me exactly what happens when I try too hard. I talk to my golf ball. I don't smile. I think a lot. I don't accept. The overall effect is that you play very, very average golf. You don't have the freedom and the flow. When I see it happening now, I cut it. Whenever I talk to a golf ball, Ronan [Flood, his caddie] will look at me and say, "There's a cuckoo around here, I'm sure there's a cuckoo around here. I'm sure there's one up in that tree." Talking to your golf ball means you are not accepting and you are trying too hard. Standing with hands on hips, arms crossed, no smile, coming off the golf course churning up – all these are signs of it. You see, I never need to try any harder. I've already given enough effort. I have to reduce how much I try in order to be a better player. That tournament at Valderrama might not be a cornerstone in my career but it's definitely one of the building blocks. That was the week the cuckoo flew.'

Though the Volvo Masters brings the European Tour season to an end, Pádraig's 2002 was far from over. He'd win twice more before Christmas: the BMW Asian Open in Taiwan followed by Tiger's Target World Challenge (presented by Williams) at Sherwood Country Club in Thousand Hills, California. Pádraig picked up a million-dollar cheque at the Target but rates that Sunday at Sherwood

Pádraig plays a shot to the 4th hole in the final round of the 2002 Target World Challenge at Sherwood Country Club, Los Angeles, going head to head with Tiger Woods.

as one of the most rewarding days in his career for a totally different reason.

'It was a big turning point,' he explains. 'Obviously I'd opened the tournament with two good rounds because I was out with Tiger on the Saturday. I shot a 63 [a course record] and played with him again in the final round. I'd been trying to figure out what the story was with all those second places and what needed to be done. I'd discussed it at length with my brother Tadhg because he's a keen student of the game, watches golfers all the time, and as a bookmaker has to keep abreast of all that's happening. So we talked about it and we set out what to do. As a direct result, I went out with a plan that Sunday at Sherwood and was determined not to deviate from it.

'I played lovely golf and was still three ahead when I hit my tee shot down fourteen. Though on the fairway, I was impeded by an overhanging tree, so I decided to hit a smooth draw shot into the middle of the green. But I hit it too hard, went long left and twenty-five yards down a bank, then just a foot or two under a fence and into the corner of a garden. Out of bounds. Tiger hit his ball in to twenty feet, so it would have been very easy to think fate was against me. Yet I walked up there thinking, "This is not good, but let's do my own thing. Keep playing my golf and see what happens" – exactly what Tadhg and I had talked about. I played a marvellous chip and putt for double-bogey and walked off the green thinking, "Right, I'm one ahead. I was unlucky to go out of bounds but let's keep playing golf. Make Tiger do his stuff."

'After we both made par at the next, a really difficult par three, I then hit two five woods on to the green at the par-five sixteenth, while Tiger was in trouble. He was still in the woods in three, over the green in four, and then, typically, chipped it in for his par. I've made birdie and gained a shot, but by chipping in it was like he'd eagled the hole. Again, I could easily have thought, "Aw no, it's happening to me again." Instead, I stayed in control of my own little world, even when he birdied the next hole.

'At the last, I hit a three iron 270 yards down the fairway. With about 160 yards to go, I hit a nine iron in there to about twenty feet. Needing to make birdie, Tiger got in trouble and made bogey. Shooting 71 was about the worst-case

Left A great iron shot to the last hole of the Target World Challenge sees Pádraig win his first individual event on US soil.

Below Pádraig holes out on the 18th in the third round of the 2003 Players Championship at the TPC Sawgrass Stadium Course, Ponte Vedra, Florida. It took a great final round by Davis Love III to push Pádraig into second place.

scenario I could come up with that day [indeed, it was equal worst of the day] but it still meant Tiger would have to shoot 64 to win, which is tough to do on command.

'That chip and putt at fourteen stand out for me, like that chip at eighteen on Sunday at Carnoustie [in 2007]. Target would be very much the time where all that started, where I first realized I didn't need good fortune or perfection or everything to go right for me; that if bad things happened I could still win. I just needed to do my thing and let it run its course. That it was Tiger made all the difference psychologically. This was his home town. Everyone wanted me to give him a run, but when it came to the crunch they wanted Tiger to win. The way I went about it that day, maintaining a steady, comfortable approach with no highs or lows, and the fact that it worked, was a massive eye-opener. If Muirfield that year had been all about focus, the Target was all about strategy, and both of them were critical in my development as a player capable of going out and winning a major.'

But Pádraig still knew the package was not yet complete. There was more great credit to be taken from his second place at the Players Championship the following April, but even though Pádraig topped the leaderboard through each of the first three rounds at Sawgrass and it took a staggering final-round 64 by Davis Love III to beat the Irishman, he admits, 'That was another occasion when I didn't truly believe I could win the tournament. Some part of me that day went out there

thinking "Hang in there," but I didn't believe I was ready to win that tournament. I know Davis had a great day and I possibly could have won, but I don't think the belief was there. As I said before, I have to go out there and really prove to myself that I can do something before actually doing it.'

He was still blessed with the ability to deliver tournament victories in Europe when they were really needed, though. After a disappointing closing 75 at The Belfry left him four strokes behind Paul Casey in the Benson and Hedges that May, Pádraig came out the following Sunday and beat Thomas Bjorn in a play-off for the Deutsche Bank SAP Open TPC of Europe at Gut Kaden.

As he continued to develop his swing, Pádraig would for long stretches concentrate on laying the foundations for his long-term future, and in 2003 he was still motivated nearly

Above Pádraig returned to winning ways at the 2003 Deutsche Bank TPC of Europe event at Gut Kaden, Hamburg, with a play-off victory over Thomas Bjorn.

as much by practice as by playing. Every so often, however, he'd think, 'It's about time I had a win,' and once he switched his mindset to tournament-winning mode, he eventually would come up trumps. 'By the time Deutsche Bank came round I needed a win,' he admits. 'As ever, I then used it as motivation, an excuse, to go back and practise.'

When it came to delivering, however, Pádraig's wife was the star that August. Determined to spend as much as possible of his first year as a father at home with Caroline and Patrick, Pádraig decided to postpone for one year (until 2005) his

application for membership of the US PGA Tour. He played well enough in the first three rounds at the BellSouth Classic in April 2004 to suggest that all-important first PGA Tour victory might soon be at hand, but he failed to perform on a frustrating final day, which would ultimately become a landmark of a different sort in his career. Though he started the final round three strokes behind his playing companion in the final group, Zach Johnson, Pádraig, then riding high at number eight in the world, 114 places ahead of the Tour rookie, was expected to put his inexperienced opponent under severe pressure. But Johnson is made of especially stern stuff, as he'd prove beyond all doubt in the 2007 US Masters, and Pádraig was out of sorts that afternoon. He could only match the youngster's level-par 72 and slipped back into fourth place.

After the tournament, I happened to be in the car park at Sugarloaf borrowing a CD or two from Pádraig's caddie Dave McNeilly for the 120-mile drive to Augusta. As we spoke, the Dubliner drove up in his large courtesy car and invited McNeilly to walk round to the driver's side for a private chat. Pádraig then drove off, uncharacteristically without even a word of farewell, and McNeilly no longer appeared to be in the mood for casual conversation. I didn't know it then, but it was the beginning of the end for one of the most enduring and popular partnerships in golf. Seven weeks later, professional golf was stunned when it finally emerged on the final day of the Deutsche Bank SAP Open TPC of Europe in Heidelberg that it would be their last together.

I and colleague Charlie Mulqueen of the *Examiner* were dismayed by McNeilly's reaction when we questioned him about their parting in the eerily silent locker-room minutes after the tournament ended. He was visibly shocked and upset. Pádraig insisted later that he'd made the situation plain to the caddie several weeks earlier, but clearly the penny hadn't dropped. McNeilly is the most professional, conscientious, hard-working, quick-witted and cheerful caddie in golf. During their six years together he'd seemed the perfect foil for Pádraig. Two guys who were prepared to go to the end of the earth in pursuit of perfection . . . and this made Pádraig's decision to end it all the more difficult for the golfing community to grasp.

'Dave was too much like me,' Pádraig explains, 'and, essentially, that's what lay behind it. His work ethic was just like mine. The whole thing was about doing more, and more, and more. We'd finish a round of golf and it'd be, "C'mon, let's go and hit golf balls. We'll work it out." Yet around that time I was trying to slow down a bit in terms of what I was doing around the golf course and I was trying to get Dave to have a slower, calmer outlook. It came to a head at BellSouth because I did get into contention; I was playing great golf; we'd done enough and didn't need to do more. I needed to take it all down, relax, take it easy; yet we

Opposite bottom Pádraig and caddie Dave McNeilly part company after the 2004 Deutsche Bank SAP Open TPC of Europe after a successful six-year partnership.

Left Pádraig with son, Paddy, during a press conference after the final round of the 2004 Deutsche Bank SAP Open TPC of Europe at St Leon-Rot, Heidelberg.

Newly appointed caddie,
Ronan Flood, helps
Pádraig to a second-place
finish in the 2004 Irish
Open at County Louth
Golf Club.

simply weren't on the same wavelength that day. I realized then it wasn't in Dave's personality to slow down and go easy. I was changing, moving on to the next phase as a player, which was being much more relaxed in myself; Dave is about getting everything done and covering all the options. It just wasn't in his psyche to move down that road with me. In the world of golf that means only one thing. It was one of the harder things I've had to do because Dave is a lovely guy, but I'm delighted to see him doing so well now with Niclas Fasth.' Pádraig is adamant that the friendship he forged with McNeilly is still intact, and it's a measure of its strength and of their mutual respect that the Ulsterman is 'the first person to text me when I win, as I text him when he has success with Niclas. Dave is a great caddie and I truly believe nobody could be keener or more supportive.'

There was even more surprise in golfing circles when Pádraig unveiled McNeilly's replacement, Ronan Flood, a good friend who was engaged to Pádraig's sister-in-law Suzanne (they'd marry three years later). Flood, a good golfer who played off a handicap of just two, originally believed he'd be back behind his desk at a bank within a few months, but it worked so well they decided to make the arrangement full-time. 'I'd one caddie in mind but didn't want to poach him off another player,' Pádraig says, 'so the idea was for Ronan to take the bag for a month or two to indicate to everybody that I was free, and caddies would come to me . . . especially the one I had my eye on. I felt I couldn't make the first approach out of loyalty to the player he was with. I knew Ronan was capable of doing the physical part of the job, but it just worked so well in every other respect. His attitude was exactly what I was looking for at that stage. It couldn't have worked out better.'

Their partnership was soon consummated, at the Linde German Masters, yet another timely victory for Pádraig, came, much to the relief of European non-playing captain Bernhard Langer, just five days before the 2004 Ryder Cup at Oakland Hills in Detroit. Pádraig came out of hibernation in 2005 at the Malaysian Open – familiar surroundings, though the Dubliner was about to open a new chapter in his career, as a full member of America's not-so-familiar PGA Tour.

'I took my card in the States because that was the next level,' he says. 'The Bell South [in 2004] hit me hard because I wanted to win in America. I thought winning the Target was big, but you've really got to go and win on the US Tour itself to establish your credentials as a player over there. So I took my card in the belief that if I played more regular events, I'd get opportunities and eventually win. I was really surprised to win so quickly.' He came from nowhere with a sensational 63 on the final day of the Honda Classic, then beat Joe Ogilvie and Vijay Singh in a play-off. It was only his fourth event of the year and his third on American soil. 'Because it meant so much to me to win in the States, because I was so focused and thinking of nothing else, out I went and got that win. When I get caught up in that mindset, things seem to happen. The 63 was spectacular [he was ten under for his first thirteen holes, for heaven's sake], but what really pleased me about the actual win was that I hit a couple of chip shots on eighteen without ever feeling under pressure or worrying about anything. I was just totally consumed by what I was doing. I was well within myself, going through my plan and playing my own game exactly like I had at the Target in 2002. I was concentrating so much on my own performance that it came as a complete shock to me when Vijay missed that short putt on the second tie hole. Mentally I was already thinking about my next tee shot.'

Revenge for that play-off defeat against Vijay in Malaysia four years earlier was 'very, very sweet', Pádraig admits. 'I felt I was due after Malaysia, and it eventually came to me. It was a very big win, very satisfying, and it came at a very significant point in my life.' Pádraig returned to Dublin on the Tuesday to discover that his

Teeing off during the final round of the 2005 Honda Classic at the Country Club at Mirasol, Palm Beach Gardens, Florida.

A play-off win over Vijay Singh and Joe Ogilvie gives Pádraig his first victory on the US Tour at the Honda Classic.

father had just had a relapse with cancer of the oesophagus. The prognosis was grim, but at least his dad had enjoyed watching his son's most significant win to date on TV. 'Oh yes, yes, he watched the whole lot of it. He cheered and jumped up out of the chair when I won. I wouldn't say it was his last piece of happiness, but he enjoyed that and really got into it. Obviously he was less able to enjoy the second one at Westchester [in June]', where Pádraig defeated Ryder Cup rival and friend Jim Furyk with a staggering sixty-five-foot putt for eagle at the final hole of the Barclays Classic. For the second time in three months he returned home from the enormous high of a tournament victory in the United States to the bleak, inescapable reality of his father's failing health. Paddy Harrington passed away a fortnight later, on the Monday of Open Championship week.

Within ten days, his son was playing at the Deutsche Bank in Gut Kaden. 'I had committed to play and just said to myself, "Look, let's go and play,"' he says. 'It wasn't tough. In fact, it's so much easier when you're on the golf course. You don't have to think or answer any questions. Always remember this: the easiest place for any golfer is on the course. We're busy and can lose ourselves out there. The hardest times are the quiet times when you're not busy doing something, especially with my dad being so close to me and with all that we did together. It's great looking back on those days we had and that things worked out the way they did. He'd be happy for me. He never needed me to win to be proud, so that was good. I never had to think like that. Yet he's a huge part of all this. His whole psyche was improving for tomorrow. He wasn't at all about today's performance, and I'm very much that way as well. It's all about who I am becoming rather than who I am now, and that was very much my dad's attitude. It's nice to have the results now, and he'd be pleased with that. In fact, I think he probably believed that was where I was going much more than I ever did.

'The strangest thing: I thought more about him when I played the Irish PGA at the European Club this summer [2007] than anywhere else. In my amateur days he was always walking the fairways, and whenever I looked around at the PGA, I half expected to see him there. I certainly felt he was there at the [2007] Open, but it's different at Carnoustie or places like that. It's definitely nice to have won those two US tournaments and to feel he saw some of the best. As it turned out he didn't get to see the absolute best, but he got to see some of it. You know, I'm sure he's enjoying it. I won't say he's proud, but I'm sure he's enjoying it.'

Paddy Harrington may not have lived to see his son scale Everest, but he gave him the gifts that made it possible, and by the end of 2005 Pádraig was ready to begin the final ascent.

The celebrations commence after an amazing sixty-five-foot breaking putt gives Pádraig his second US Tour victory at the 2005 Barclays Classic, New York.

Easy Ryder

Charlie Mulqueen

THE COUNTRY CLUB, BROOKLINE, 1999

Pádraig Harrington's Ryder Cup odyssey might very well have begun at Valderrama in 1997, but it could just as easily have been delayed until The Belfry in 2002. He had been a professional golfer for a mere two years in 1997, but a series of fine performances, including that closing round of 67 in The Open Championship at Royal Troon for a share of fifth place, kept him on the fringes of the top ten and an automatic spot on the team throughout the campaign.

The build-up to the completion of that particular side was dominated by a much-publicized row between the captain Seve Ballesteros and his Spanish compatriot Miguel Martín. Seve clearly didn't want Martín in the team, seeing his old sparring partner José-María Olázabal (who was well back in the points ranking) as a far more suitable candidate. So when Martín picked up a wrist injury that sidelined him for a few weeks late in the season, Ballesteros saw his opportunity and struck as ruthlessly as he had so often done on the golf course itself. Medical opinion didn't seem to matter; Seve deemed Martín unfit for the Ryder Cup, and that was that. Olázabal would play. No further argument.

Back in Ireland, Pádraig watched the contretemps with no great fascination. His task was to build on a splendid Open Championship and six other top ten finishes. He was still in contention when the final counting tournament of the year, the BMW International at the Nord-Eichenried course just outside Munich, came round. The difficulty for Pádraig was that the event invariably developed into a birdie-fest and no matter how good you might score yourself, the chances were that

somebody else would outshoot you. That was very much the case in 1997: his nineteen-under-par 269 for the seventy-two holes finished no better than tied ninth. Two strokes fewer and he would have been in the side at Valderrama. And the likelihood is that he would have been a valuable member of Seve's side: later in the year Pádraig partnered Paul McGinley to win the World Cup for Ireland for the first time in thirty-nine years at Kiawah Island, and finished eighth in the European Tour Order of Merit.

'I nearly made the European Ryder Cup team back in 1997 at a time when it was first confirmed that the match was coming to Ireland,' Pádraig recalls. 'That was great news and helped to ease my disappointment at not making the side. And in truth I was still a little inexperienced at that time and probably better off to have waited for Brookline two years later.' Still, there was a lot of agonizing and nervousness before his place in that 1999 side was assured. In fact it was in considerable doubt with two tournaments still to be played: the now defunct West of Ireland Open at Galway Bay and the BMW International in Munich. The prize money at stake in Galway was relatively low by top European standards, but the official points he picked up there were to prove crucial. On the final day he had a chance of overtaking Costantino Rocca until driving out of bounds on the 16th,

An eight-foot putt on the final hole of the 1999 BMW International at the Golfclub München, Munich, clinches second place for Pádraig and, more importantly, his first Ryder Cup spot.

and in those circumstances he did extremely well to hold on for second place.

Onward, then, to Munich, where fate this time round was poised to lend Pádraig a more favourable hand. After three rounds it was apparent that second place on his own would earn him the coveted spot, and that looked a very sound bet as he entered the final eighteen on equal terms with Colin Montgomerie at the top of the leaderboard with his nearest challengers some way off the pace. However, the butterflies were extremely restless in the Harrington tummy early on that lovely sunny Sunday morning, and he quickly found himself four over par after as many holes. The Ryder Cup dream was on the point of being shattered, but to his enormous credit he fought back in style and was even par for the day by the time he reached the 18th tee.

The green at this par five is comfortably reachable in two shots, but trouble abounds on both sides of the fairway, and a water hazard to the right of the green and sand to the left threaten an overly bold approach. Those damned butterflies fluttered again, and Pádraig didn't exactly play the hole to the manner born. Eventually he was left with an eight-footer for par. As he prepared to take his stance, he looked back at his wife, Caroline, and me standing anxiously some thirty yards away and asked if he had to hole this putt to be sure of the team place. At the time we believed he had to make par, so we signalled that, yes, it needed to go in. Bravely and skilfully, he hit a beautiful left-to-right putt into the dead centre of the cup. He threw his arms in the air the way champions normally do, even though on this occasion Montgomerie was a clear three-stroke winner of the tournament. Caroline and I hugged and danced, and as bad luck would have it the Sky cameras caught us in the act. The cynics in the press tent immediately dubbed me 'Caroline's surrogate father', and it stuck for a while, but parents Dermot and Mary at home in Dublin, watching nervously on television, weren't complaining!

A mountain had been scaled so far as Pádraig's career was concerned, and he was a proud man a few weeks later as he climbed aboard Concorde and headed for Boston and the Country Club in Brookline. It was to be one of the most controversial weeks in the game's history but, typical of the man, Pádraig kept out of the shenanigans, concentrating instead on doing his job for the team to the very best of his ability.

'Naturally, I will never forget my first match in the Ryder Cup,' he says. 'I wasn't supposed to play on the first morning, but José-María Olázabal felt his game had gone off the boil so I was drafted in as partner to Miguel-Angel Jiménez. And, you know, I still rate him my favourite Ryder Cup partner. He was playing the best golf of his life at that time. I remember his tee shot at the first left me with a seven iron

Pádraig and foursomes partner, Miguel-Angel Jiménez, secure a half with Davis Love III and Payne Stewart in the first-day foursomes of the 1999 Ryder Cup at The Country Club, Brookline, Boston, USA.

Pádraig claims a one-hole victory over Mark O'Meara in the final-day singles at Brookline.

to the green. But I was so nervous I could hardly see the ball. Having stood there for what must have seemed like an age, I told myself, "You've got to hit it now." It was very much a swing purely by memory.

'We halved that match, and by the time the singles came round I was over the worst of the nerves. I went out against Mark O'Meara, the former Open champion, and my focus was really good. Through the back nine I could see the crowds swelling and people shouting at O'Meara that they badly needed this match, so I knew the overall picture was really tight. I remember our captain Mark James was waiting for me on the sixteenth and he was as white as a sheet. I kept my head down. I was excited. I hit the best shot of my life into that green. O'Meara put his in a bunker and bogeyed to give me a one-hole lead, which I held.

'I'll never forget the atmosphere. It was like standing beside the sound system in a disco, it was that noisy. The galleries were ten deep and they were all roaring at Mark and chanting "USA, USA, go for it, Mark!" and that kind of stuff and putting him under a lot of pressure. I hit a great drive down the last, a par four of 480 yards. I was 154 yards from the flag but I was so pumped up I played a wedge for my second. I won my match and was as high as a kite. I've just won my match and also believe I've won the Ryder Cup! I don't think my feet touched the ground as I ran back to the seventeenth green. And just as I settled down, Justin Leonard holed *that* putt.

'The disappointment in the European camp was acute, and the television and the papers were full of what happened on that green. But I had no problem with it; indeed, it says a lot for European golf that the Americans should have reacted like they did. It showed how much winning the Ryder Cup meant to them, and it should also be appreciated that they staged an amazing recovery that day.' Ben Crenshaw's side went into the final day's singles 10–6 down; by the end of play Europe had lost the match 14½–13½.

Pádraig has become hugely popular in the United States for a combination of reasons – that ready, flashing smile, his good humour and his willingness to stand there and sign autograph after autograph being only a few of them. Nevertheless, some Americans believed he played just a little too slowly in his match against O'Meara. After he had walked ninety yards up to the green prior to playing his second shot at the 17th, NBC commentator Dick Enberg observed that this 'gave new meaning to the Boston marathon', although Harrington contends that it was probably the most important shot of his life up to that point.

Present in the gallery that day were a number of family members, including Pádraig's parents Paddy and Breda, two of the greatest supporters any sportsman could have. Paddy, of course, has since sadly passed on, but he imbued his son with some wonderful character traits and they were on display in the sporting and rational manner in which he accepted the enormous disappointment of Brookline 1999.

Wild celebrations greet Justin Leonard's putt on the 17th green at Brookline, as the USA stage an amazing last-day recovery to beat Europe by a single point.

THE BELFRY, 2002

The events of 9/11 meant that the 2001 match had to be postponed for twelve months. It was, of course, a decision everybody understood and accepted. It was also agreed that the two teams would remain unchanged so that there were no real losers. Except that Pádraig Harrington played some of the finest golf of his career in 2001, capping it all by winning the Volvo Masters at Montecastillo at the end of the season and finishing second in the Order of Merit behind the relentless Colin Montgomerie. However, he was far from happy with his form when battle was finally joined once more in September 2002.

'I played the first match with Niclas Fasth,' Pádraig recalls, 'a guy I would always like as a partner in that kind of format. He's a one hundred per cent battler and

Pádraig agonizes after missing a putt at the 18th hole to halve the hole during the first day of the 2002 Ryder Cup at The Belfry. Partnering Niclas Fasth they lose the match one down to Phil Mickelson and David Toms.

never gives up. But I lost my first two matches, with Niclas and Paul McGinley, and felt I was playing very poorly. So I went to Sam Torrance, our captain, and asked him to stand me down so that I could get in a morning's practice.

'I went out in the afternoon fourballs on the second day with Monty. He was playing well so I knew all I had to do was keep him in good spirits. My sole goal was to keep him happy, keep telling jokes. He just thought my caddie Dave McNeilly and I were the weirdest people he ever came across because of what we talked about going around the course. One of the things we were trying to figure out was how much money Monty would have made if he got a dollar for every time he hit that three wood of his that he used to play off the tee. Then we were trying to figure it out in electricity currency – I think it is UMHs – all sorts of things; we were working out energy levels needed and all that sort of stuff. We were winding him up, trying to keep him happy. As I say, I knew he was playing well and that in fourballs if I threw in a few birdies and played erratically, which I did, he would play the solid golf and we'd be fine. And we were, beating Phil Mickelson and David Toms by 2&1.

'This may sound a little daft, but my singles the following day against Mark Calcavecchia was the best game of golf of my life. I was playing rubbish but I got myself really psyched up, which you have to do in matchplay. I did so by telling myself that this guy was really going to rip me apart because I was playing so badly and that he was a streaky player and would go out and birdie the first nine holes.

So I went out there in the best frame of mind focus-wise that I could ever be. I remember hitting it in the water at the eighth – probably the ugliest tee shot I've ever hit in golf. Yet I walked off the tee and told Dave McNeilly that it was the shot that was going to win me the match. I knew I was going to hit bad shots that day. I was prepared to take my punishment.

'The eighth was playing into the wind and it was difficult. With me in the water off the tee, Calcavecchia probably did the right thing and played down the right-hand side. But when he didn't hit the fairway, I knew he wasn't going to make four.

I took my penalty drop and put a wood into a greenside bunker. He missed the green, chipped up and missed the putt, and I got up and down for a half. That broke his heart. He was two down at that stage and that was the nail in his coffin. I know I holed a raker at the ninth, where the ball was going so fast that it jumped up in the air and fell in, but that wasn't as significant as the eighth. That bogey was definitely the winning of the match. He was gone. When you can't win a hole after your opponent has played the kind of tee shot I hit at the eighth, you don't feel you're going to win any holes. He couldn't see any way out of it.

'I walked on to the thirteenth green having knocked it to ten feet and thought, "It's amazing how well I'm playing considering how badly I'm swinging the club." I hit it close a lot of times. I practised well into the dark the night before. It was pitch dark. I'd have one divot going miles right and the next divot going miles left. It was just horrible. There was no figuring out what I was doing, and bear in mind I won the Dunhill the following week with the same swing!

'Anyway, back to the thirteenth. I had that ten-footer to go five up with five to play, and if the match had finished there only ten or so people would have been watching. Everybody had left. McGinley had started what was to be the most fateful round of his career, and once I'd got through nine holes and was three or four up, I hit it real close at ten, eleven and twelve and just lagged my putts. My whole idea was, don't let him in, don't let him in, because I was so afraid of him. You could see all the Irish people drift away they were so bored with it all.

'I got to see a lot of golf that afternoon. I was second match to finish after Monty and it was an exciting Ryder Cup to be watching. Best of all, of course, was when Paul holed the winning putt on the final green. It was a huge moment, but I've often wondered why he celebrated by diving into the lake. Seriously, though, the way Paul finished it off and the circumstances made it really exciting.'

OAKLAND HILLS, 2004

Europe might have captured the Ryder Cup for the third time in four matches, but European chief executive Ken Schofield wasn't satisfied. He recognized the need to alter the team's

Pádraig acknowledges the crowd on the 9th hole at The Belfry during his 5&4 singles win over Mark Calcavecchia.

selection process. Increasing numbers of his top players were plying their trade on the PGA Tour in the US and might not qualify for the team under the old system. The change he advocated was that five places should be chosen off the world rankings and five from the domestic circuit, along with the customary two wildcards. When the erudite Schofield wanted something, he usually got his way, and in 2004 it duly transpired that Pádraig along with Sergio Garcia, Darren Clarke, Miguel-Angel Jiménez and Lee Westwood made the team as a result of their world ranking status.

In terms of the Ryder Cup, the Americans were reeling. They couldn't really get their heads around what was happening. A quick look at the world rankings told you that there really shouldn't be a contest: the USA team possessed some of the game's greatest, most of them in their prime, such as Tiger Woods, Phil Mickelson, Davis Love III and Jim Furyk. All sorts of theories were doing the rounds in search of an explanation for the Americans' failings – and their Ryder Cup misery was set to become only greater.

'One of the great thrills I've had in my three Ryder Cup matches was the opener in 2004 at Oakland Hills when Monty and I took on the so-called dream team of Tiger and Phil,' says Pádraig. 'People were claiming we hadn't a hope against them, but who couldn't get pumped up for a challenge like that? We were ready. We won the first hole and never looked back. It was after that match that all the publicity

Below left The scoreboard tells the story of the opening-day fourball matches in the 2004 Ryder Cup at Oakland Hills, Detroit, USA, as Europe take a commanding lead.

Below right Pádraig teams up with Colin Montgomerie to defeat Tiger Woods and Phil Mickelson 2&1 in the opening-day fourball match at Oakland Hills.

began about how Tiger and Phil didn't like each other and didn't get on. There was a famous TV picture of Tiger's startled face after Phil launched a really wayward drive at a crucial stage late in the match that people believed told its own story. In fairness, though, it's very difficult for two top players to play together. You can't see one of them being the leader and telling the other guy, "This is what we're going to do: we're going to give this putt and we're not going to give that one," and so on. It's not easy for anyone in that kind of situation.'

The early indications were that Europe were running away with it, although that could have changed somewhat on Saturday morning had Paul Casey and David Howell not been able to pull off a sensational final-green victory over Chad Campbell and Jim Furyk in the second session of fourballs. That result seemed to shatter American resolve just as it imbued the Europeans with ever-increasing confidence.

Partnering Colin Montgomerie, Pádraig hits a tee shot during their second-day fourball match at Oakland Hills against Stewart Cink and Davis Love III, which they lost 3&2.

'I partnered McGinley in the foursomes on that Saturday afternoon,' Pádraig continues. 'I started badly and we were two down early on against Tiger and Davis. It wasn't looking good at all and Paul had to have a word with me. It's the only time I think I've ever listened to him, and he was right. I just wasn't up for it. Thankfully I got into the flow of the match and it turned into an easy day for us, which was incredible to be honest. It was a great Irish occasion. Paul and I have Irish caddies, Darren Reynolds and Ronan Flood, and their families and a huge number of Irish people waving tricolours danced and sang after we won on the fifteenth green. They were entitled to do so. It was massive to beat Tiger and Davis by 4&3. They kept pushing but could do little right after they fell behind.'

A fascinating feature of the Oakland Hills encounter was Bernhard Langer's captaincy. In traditional Germanic fashion he had ensured that every last detail, no matter how tiny, was attended to, while his advice on the golf course proved invaluable. Pádraig was chosen to hit the tee shots at the odd holes in the foursomes matches, and these included each of the four par threes. 'Bernhard came up to me on each tee and told me the club to play, the place to hit it and why I should hit it there,' says Pádraig. 'While it wasn't exactly like he was demanding that you should do it, you were definitely aware of what he wanted you to do.' Reflecting on the week some time later, Langer explained his strategy. 'It helps the

....

Captain Bernhard Langer
marshals his team
to a conclusive victory
at Oakland Hills, as
Europe win by a record
nine points.

players to have a second opinion from someone they respect,' he said. 'If they have a doubt and you tell them to take such a club and aim for a certain spot, they will think, "That's what I was going to do anyway," and in turn it fires up their confidence.'

Because of the magnificent way the Americans had rallied at Brookline in 1999, nobody began to count European chickens just yet, although with a lead of 11–5 going into the final day they needed only 3½ points from the twelve singles for victory. As it transpired, Hal Sutton and his team were demoralized and let themselves down pretty badly. Tiger won his match at number one against Paul Casey and played very well, but he still came in for a deal of stick for his overall contribution to his team's cause – something Pádraig believes was more than a little unfair. 'It's very hard for a guy who manages himself every week quite differently to everyone else to be told, "Look, you're playing a practice round that will take five hours at a certain point in the day instead of a practice round for three hours at six o'clock in the morning,"' he reasons. 'Tiger also has to do this interview and that interview which he wouldn't have to do in a normal week.

'On the Sunday I was out at the end of the field, and by the time I reached the fourteenth the outcome had been decided. I was two up on Jay Haas at the time and really struggled to play any golf after that. Two things happened in that match: at the first hole I hit an appalling tee shot; at the second I stood up and hit the best drive of my life. I was so proud of myself that I didn't let that first shot upset me. I then hit my approach to six feet at the second, and that gave me tremendous self-belief and confidence.

'I don't agree with playing out when the overall result has been decided. I think it should be called a half and off you go. But eventually I holed a big putt on the eighteenth to beat Haas. It meant I had won all my singles matches in the Ryder Cup so far, and you want to maintain that kind of record, but you'd be amazed at what goes through your head in a Ryder Cup situation. There's a release of tension when the overall result has been decided and your game doesn't count any more. I won most of those matches because I got hyped up over them. I've always been a disaster without pressure. It totally went that day after the fourteenth.'

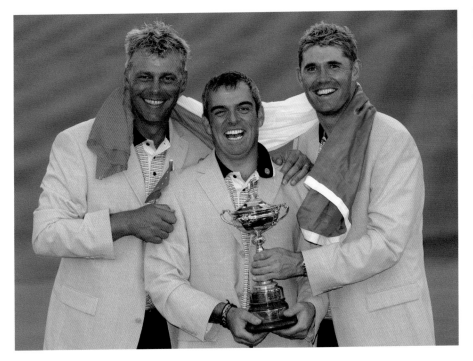

European teammates
Darren Clarke, Paul
McGinley and Pádraig
celebrate the victory at
Oakland Hills.

Be that as it may, the Harrington–McGinley axis came good once again, Langer demonstrating both his cunning and willingness to listen to advice. Conscious that a massive Irish crowd had been turning up all week, Caroline Harrington came up with the idea that Pádraig and Paul should play in successive matches to harness that support in the event of a close-run finish. At 18½–9½ it was far from that, but both still won their matches in the European romp.

Champagne sprayed and flowed, Irish ballads roared out into the blue Detroit skies, and Harrington, McGinley and Clarke were famously photographed under the tricolour. Between them they had contributed nine points to the European cause. Meanwhile, Langer was prophesying that 'the party of all parties' would take place two years hence in Ireland. We could hardly wait.

THE K CLUB, 2006

For a period of time there was a possibility that Pádraig would not actually play his way into the European team for the 2006 renewal of the Ryder Cup at The K Club – an occasion he and the rest of Ireland had been savouring for several years. That wouldn't have pleased skipper Ian Woosnam. It was unthinkable that one of his two precious wildcards might have to go to a player deemed essential to the

European cause. It was not part of Woosie's gameplan. In an effort to avoid that happening, Pádraig took in the French Open, a tournament endowed with copious Ryder Cup points but one he had never before been able to slot into his schedule. He birdied the last two holes on the final afternoon to finish second, a shot behind John Bickerton, and more or less clinch his spot. Paul McGinley worked his socks off to make it, and when Darren Clarke received one of Woosie's wildcards, the Big Three were there for the third successive Ryder Cup to increase the massive hype surrounding the competition in the host country. 'You don't like to make too much of these things in public,' Pádraig commented, 'but I'm very proud for myself and my family that I'm playing in the Ryder Cup for the fourth successive match. I know Paul and Darren feel very much the same way, and it certainly is great for Ireland to have three of our players in the side for the third successive match.'

Even as he spoke, the rain was coming down in sheets, threatening everybody's enjoyment of the proceedings and prompting Pádraig to express the fervent wish that 'the weather brightens up and the fans can enjoy themselves as we'd all like them to do. And hopefully we can play our part by giving them something to cheer.' But the weather didn't relent. It rained and it blew throughout the week, except for the opening ceremony, the final-afternoon singles and the triumphant closing party. Nevertheless, 40,000 Irish men and women turned out on each of the practice days and for the match itself to ring true Langer's prophetic words. It was indeed some hooley!

As for giving the fans something to cheer about, the Europeans, and most especially Darren Clarke, really came up trumps. He had lost his lovely wife Heather to cancer only six weeks earlier and wasn't even sure if he should have been at

Pádraig hits Europe's opening tee shot at the 2006 Ryder Cup at The K Club, Ireland, during his fourball match partnering Colin Montgomerie against Tiger Woods and Jim Furyk, a match they lost one down.

The K Club. It was to the great credit of the big man from Dungannon that he got through the week so well. His eyes clearly welled with tears as he made his way to the first tee on the opening morning, but his friend and fourball partner Lee Westwood and faithful caddie Billy Foster helped him through it, so well that Darren actually birdied the opening hole. He hit a marvellous drive, followed with an approach to about eight feet, and nonchalantly rolled in the putt. He went on to win each of his three matches. 'It was always going to be emotional for me this morning, especially on the first tee,' he said of that opening encounter. 'It was great to have Lee there helping me through. I'll never forget the reception the crowd gave me. Lee and our opponents Phil Mickelson and Chris DiMarco hugged me, and it was a very special moment, very touching. That's what the Ryder Cup is all about. It's not about animosity, it's a match among friends that we both want to win. All the American team have shown me great sympathy this week, and it's very nice and kind of them. I got a lot of hugs at the end today and I was feeling emotions that hopefully you don't ever have to feel.'

In truth, the Ryder Cup in Ireland as an actual golfing contest never seriously materialized, nor did it ever look like doing so. Tiger Woods hooked his opening drive into the lake not long before Clarke birdied the hole. That set a trend that was never reversed. Europe led by a point after that session, which saw Pádraig and Monty beaten on the 18th by Woods and Jim Furyk. The gap was stretched by another point in the afternoon when the Irish pairing of Harrington and McGinley halved with Chad Campbell and Zach Johnson. Even though Pádraig lost again in the second-morning foursomes alongside Henrik Stenson against Scott Verplank and Johnson, Europe cruised further into the lead, taking the session 2½–1½. It developed into a rout that afternoon as Paul Casey holed in one at the 14th to finish off his match with David Howell against Stewart Cink and Johnson. Pádraig was playing nice golf but not getting the breaks, and this time he and McGinley went down to the top American pairing of Woods and Furyk 3&2.

So Europe entered the final day leading 10–6 and needing only four points from the twelve singles to retain the trophy, plus another half-point to win again for the fourth time in five matches. The only issue to be resolved that Sunday was identifying clearly who it was who sank the winning putt. Depending on your point of view, it was Henrik Stenson or David Howell, but unfortunately not Darren Clarke. Ian Woosnam had placed him at number seven in the order, suspecting that might be the spot to ensure such an

Pádraig narrowly misses a putt on the 10th green during the morning fourball match at The K Club.

eventuality. Darren won all right, amid incredible emotion, on the 16th green, but it was a minute or two too late.

As Pádraig has always maintained, his competitive juices cease to flow once there's nothing left to play for, and this was very much the case in his match with Verplank. The American stuck to his guns though, and recorded a hole in one at the 13th – the sixth in the cup's history – in his 4&3 win. Pádraig wouldn't dream of making excuses and had little to apologize for anyway because he played nice golf through the week; it was just that the ball rarely bounced in his favour, or else his opponents were right on their game. And Verplank had a point to prove. Although one of captain Tom Lehman's wildcard picks, he had been given only one match prior to the singles, which he won, and he was in the American team room when television analyst Johnny Miller described him as 'deadwood'. That hurt Verplank and galvanized him into playing some of the best golf of the week.

But his efforts didn't save the USA team from a second successive humiliation, 18½–9½ – the exact same score as at Oakland Hills two years earlier. It would almost certainly have been another half-point more had Paul McGinley not conceded a twenty-foot putt to level the match on the 18th after his opponent J. J. Henry was distracted by a streaker as he stood over the ball. That gesture earned Paul a mild rebuke from Woosnam, who would have liked to win it by a record margin. It also served to underline the Irishman's superb sporting instincts.

Pádraig, and especially his caddie Ronan Flood, celebrated as wildly as everybody else on the roof of the clubhouse, Guinness and champagne the order of the day. It took the players and the exuberant fans quite a time to come down from the excitement of it all. Pádraig had taken a mere half-point from his five Ryder Cup matches, but he wasn't allowing that statistic to worry him. All he had ever really desired was for his team to win the Ryder Cup in his native country, and for the occasion to be a massive success. So he was entirely satisfied with the way things panned out. For more than a year he had been the public face of the Ryder Cup in Ireland. You couldn't walk down the street, switch on your radio and television or go through airports and railway stations, even public toilets, without seeing that familiar smile beaming out at you and telling you how good the Ryder Cup was going to be in Ireland. Nothing could dampen his spirits or cause him to do anything other than enjoy such a massive occasion on his native heath. Notably, despite the fact that he hadn't won a tournament in fifteen months, Pádraig captured the Alfred Dunhill Links Championship a fortnight later with his amateur partner and friend J. P. McManus, and ended the season as European number one.

'As a player, I did what I could,' he reflected on that crushing victory over the Americans, 'although I probably should have played better than I did in the first-morning fourballs with Monty. After that I stuck to my guns and have no regrets.

I came up against it in a few matches and didn't hole the putts at the right time. There had been such a build-up all year, indeed for the last six years, that it was a huge relief that we won. I would have hated to lose the Ryder Cup in Ireland. As long as the team won, it didn't matter who got the points. It would be no consolation if I won my five matches and the team lost. It would be very disappointing if I only got a half-point and the team lost by that margin. I might have been gutted in those circumstances. I honestly couldn't have tried or worked any harder. I couldn't have been more disciplined or had a better attitude. All those things I was good at, so I can't have any complaints at all.'

Another factor that delighted Pádraig about the Ryder Cup in Ireland was the favourable reaction of the American players to the week, and especially how fairly they were treated by the fans. As Tiger Woods told him, 'They were incredible, the best I've ever seen. They were the fairest, the most appreciative I've ever encountered at the Ryder Cup. These people know their golf.'

Who can foretell what future Ryder Cups hold for Pádraig Harrington? He loves the week passionately, though he admits he's glad it's a biennial affair because the pressure and demands are massive, with so much happening on and off the golf course. For sure, a European team without Pádraig and his marvellously supportive wife Caroline is unimaginable right now.

Pádraig and the rest of the team party during the closing ceremony at The K Club after a convincing win by nine points for the second consecutive time.

Strictly on merit

Brian Keogh

He was fifty yards away, but he had the scent in his nostrils and wouldn't stop until he had his quarry at his mercy. With the instincts of a hunter, he covered the short distance separating him from his objective and let fly for the first time in five long years. 'Five double Whoppers with fries and five Cokes, por favor,' he said, trying his best not to drool as he stared at the menu with that wide-eyed look that would become all too familiar to those who would watch him snaffle the Irish Open, the Irish Professional Championship and then The Open Championship (from another Spaniard) just a matter of months later.

With the Harry Vardon Trophy in his carry-on luggage, Pádraig had physical evidence that he had just achieved one of his career ambitions: he'd claimed the European Tour's Order of Merit title with the sweetest second-place finish of his life, in the 2006 Volvo Masters at Valderrama. He felt he deserved a treat. 'We dashed from Valderrama to the airport thinking we were late, but there were around a hundred people in the queue to check in and near the check-in desk there was a fast-food burger joint. There were three of us, I think – Caroline, Ronan and me – and I bought five double Whoppers. I hadn't eaten a fast-food burger in five years, but I ate two there on the spot, and never were burgers enjoyed as much as those ones were. I think as I walked back with all these burgers and chips and Cokes, everybody was aghast, looking at me with all this fast food. That was my celebration at winning the Order of Merit. I fully understood after this why people enjoy fast food. At the right time, nothing tastes as good. It was just delicious.'

Opposite Pádraig and partner, J. P. McManus, celebrate their victory in the 2006 Dunhill Links Championship team event, the start of a special period in Pádraig's career.

Since he'd faded on the back nine to lose the thirty-six-hole 2001 Cisco World Match Play final to Ian Woosnam at Wentworth, Pádraig had continued to rack up the second-place finishes until the tally stood at twenty-nine. After Woosnam handed him his sixteenth runner-up spot that day, the Dubliner could not hide his disgust and made immediate plans to improve his winning ratio. His hunger for victory grew sharper than ever. 'Finishing second in a tournament can be a great performance,' he observed after Woosnam had come back from three down early in the afternoon round to win 2&1, 'but in an individual event, when I'm second it does bother me. It looks like I don't like to finish the job off. I'm certainly not finishing it off. Something must change down the home stretch. Disappointed is not the word for how I feel about today. Disgusted is the word. The ball was in my court and it was totally my fault that he was not under pressure playing the back nine. I lost concentration. "Why?" is the unanswered question. I can't always say I got unlucky or that someone else did something. It is up to me to do something. I'm reasonably patient, but I am beginning to lose my patience about this.'

Five years later, at Valderrama, Pádraig was able to celebrate his thirtieth career second place. It was Jeev Milkha Singh who raised the trophy among the cork oaks, but Pádraig felt like the real winner after producing the goods down the home stretch to earn enough cash to edge out Paul Casey by €35,252 and mark this important milestone on the road to major championship glory at Carnoustie the following summer.

It was a journey that had begun in earnest on the links courses of Scotland just a few weeks earlier, when he romped home by the biggest winning margin of his career in the Alfred Dunhill Links Championship. Victory by five shots at St Andrews – his most comfortable win since his maiden professional victory in the 1996 Spanish Open in Madrid – suddenly put Pádraig within touching distance of the Order of Merit title and gave him a realistic chance of erasing the disappointment of finishing second best to Retief Goosen in 2001 and 2002.

Of course, Harrington's ultimate triumph in the Order of Merit owed much to his battle to rack up qualifying points consistently and secure his fourth Ryder Cup appearance at The K Club. But as things turned out, the Dubliner did not gather enough points to secure his place until he had made the cut in the BMW International in Munich.

By the time he got to Carton House for the Nissan Irish Open in May he admitted that if something didn't give, he would be lucky to scrape into the team and subsequently set out to make his Ryder Cup points from eight tournaments: the US Open, French Open, Smurfit European Open, The Open, Deutsche Bank TPC, US PGA, WGC-Bridgestone Invitational and the BMW International.

Three closing bogeys in the US Open at Winged Foot left Pádraig wondering what might have been as Geoff Ogilvy finished two shots ahead of him to win his first major title. Yet there was a silver lining to Harrington's cloud in the shape of more than 200,000 Ryder Cup points.

Having finished second in the Booz Allen Classic in a Monday finish the following week, Harrington jetted to Paris for the French Open and racked up the twenty-eighth second place of his career to move up to sixth position in the qualifying race as the leading player from the European Points List.

His presence at The K Club looked certain with five big-money events coming up in July and August, yet he contrived to make life stressful by missing the cut in both The Open at Hoylake and the US PGA Championship at Medinah in Chicago.

As he entered the final counting event in Munich, it was still mathematically possible for him to be bumped from the side, should he miss the cut again. But he made a mockery of pessimistic predictions by finishing second for the twenty-ninth time in his career – Henrik Stenson's eagle three at the first hole of a sudden-death play-off closing the door on Pádraig and Retief Goosen.

Fourth place in the Madrid Open the week before the Ryder Cup confirmed Pádraig's status as a serious contender for the Order of Merit, and a disappointing per-sonal performance at The K Club and a stale showing in the American Express Championship at The Grove simply sharpened his desire to do the business when he arrived at St Andrews for the Alfred Dunhill Links Championship.

Pádraig plays out of a bunker during the final round of the Dunhill Links Championship at the Old Course, St Andrews, clinching the individual title by five shots.

'I came into the Dunhill Links off the [2006] Ryder Cup, and obviously the tremendous thing about the Ryder Cup in Ireland was winning it,' Pádraig recalled. 'I had a very average week at The K Club myself, only winning half a point. I had a very average performance in general. It was almost stale in some ways because I just didn't hole the putts or raise my game enough to win the matches. It was a little bit of a kick up the backside for me, and I went into the Alfred Dunhill Links Championship and just played the golf. Many times in my career I have used poor performances to spur me on. A barren spell always gets me going, and I probably had a bit of a barren spell going into that Ryder Cup in terms of wins. I didn't do much wrong, but I didn't do much right either, so the Dunhill was a big positive for me.

'I probably had the tournament won with nine holes to go. All the way through I hit the shots. I remember I did hit a lovely four iron into the sixteenth from a long way left, and, like a lot of shots that day, I struck the ball well. It was one of those good days when everything went as planned. There were no hiccups, and I definitely walked away from it feeling very confident about my game. But like a lot of my wins, it was a case of push comes to shove. That's what makes me do it.'

Having J. P. McManus as his pro-am partner proved to be a fillip for Pádraig, who was sufficiently distracted by the team standings not to brood on any poor shots of his own. 'In the Dunhill,' he said, 'I definitely have an advantage over the field, there is no question about that. There is a pick-me-up at the Dunhill, a good atmosphere. I enjoyed my whole week there, and I think it helps on the golf course when you enjoy a particular tournament and everything going on around it. Things like that push me along – when I have something else to push for rather than just myself. I can sometimes be quite content in what I am doing, in working forward and playing my game and improving my game. And while that is all very well, it is not the best method for getting the best out of your game in a given week. It may be good in the long term, but sometimes my goals aren't short-term enough and I get caught up in focusing for down the road and the immediate future.'

Until this point in his career, Pádraig had often been accused of believing that there were no tomorrows in terms of planning his route to the top. After finishing somewhere in the middle of the pack, he would often declare himself to be delighted with his game, to the frustration of many. There was always something to work on before he was ready, another aspect of his game that needed attention. He'd often find himself on a practice ground honing an element of his game for some fog-shrouded moment in the distant future. A fresh policy of total focus on the job at hand, however, soon began to pay dividends, and his win in the 2006 Dunhill Links immediately brought the race for the Order of Merit sharply into focus. Victory at St Andrews moved Pádraig up three places to second on the Order of Merit, just €218,185 behind Ryder Cup teammate Casey, and suddenly the post-Ryder Cup blues had been banished and there was a new urgency in his game and a spring in his step.

In an attempt to cut the gap on Casey to manageable proportions, Pádraig hastily made plans to play in the Mallorca Classic at Pula two weeks later but missed the cut by three shots. Yet playing the week before a major event – as he would prove with his victory in the Irish Professional Championship the week before The Open – has never been a bad thing for Pádraig Harrington.

Though he was comfortable with his game, Jaime Patiño's Spanish masterpiece had never been kind to Pádraig in the past. True, he'd won the Volvo Masters in 2001, but that victory came at Montecastillo in Jerez, not on the manicured but claustrophobic Valderrama course, where his best finish was a share of tenth place behind his close friend Paul McGinley the previous season. Ominously, he had gone to Valderrama with a better chance of winning the Order of Merit in 2002, when he cut the gap on Retief Goosen to just €23,119 but could only finish tied for thirty-sixth, a stroke behind the South African. Fortunately, the mathematical permutations this time round left him in no doubt as to what he had to do: win the tournament and the Order of Merit title was definitely his.

Unfortunately for Casey, the Englishman suffered a stomach bug early in the week and needed an injection midway through an opening round of 76; he eventually rallied to finish tied for twenty-first. His struggles left the door open for Pádraig, who now knew that second place would be good enough. But having stumbled to a 72 on Saturday, Pádraig was tied for thirteenth place going into the final round and was faced with the possibility of finishing second in the Order of Merit for the third time in his career. England's David Howell and Sweden's Robert

Pádraig faces questions during a press conference in advance of the 2006 Volvo Masters at Valderrama, Cadiz.

Pádraig plays his pitch to the 72nd at Valderrama, managing to hole the par putt to finish second at the Volvo Masters.

Karlsson could still win the event and sneak the title themselves, so Pádraig knew that he needed the putting round of his life. Still, second place was a big ask with so many players between him and the top of the leaderboard.

Before the week had even started, he'd said, 'I've got to go out there and win it so I've been focusing on trying to do my best this week to get myself up near the top and be in contention with nine to go. If you're in contention with nine holes to go anything can happen.' As it turned out he did put himself in the mix with nine holes to go. He had a remarkable day on the greens, even by his own high standards. By finishing with eight single putts in a row, he shot 69 and ended up in a three-way tie for second with Sergio Garcia and Luke Donald.

So Pádraig Harrington stood proudly at the summit of European golf as successor to Colin Montgomerie; but it had been a white-knuckle ride right to the end. Having hauled himself up to third place with birdies at the 4th, 11th, 14th and 16th, he looked to have thrown all the hard work away by pulling his four-iron approach into the water at the perilous par-five 17th that had been so controversially re-designed by Seve Ballesteros for the 1997 Ryder Cup matches. With the ball in the water, his odds on becoming European number one soared to 40–1 with online bookmakers, but he managed to get up and down for par, holing from eight feet. As an encore he produced an even more stunning par save at the last that was to prove crucial in his bid to become the third Irish winner of the Vardon Trophy after Christy O'Connor Sr in 1961 and 1962 and Ronan Rafferty in 1989. In trouble off the tee, he was still sixty-two yards from the pin in two but pitched to four feet from the rough and rolled in his twenty-fourth putt of the day to post a one-under-par total of 283.

The Dubliner then headed to the players' lounge with Caroline, his three-year-old son Paddy and members of his extended family to endure an agonizing sixty-minute wait to see if Garcia and Singh would deny him the second place he needed to become Europe's number one for the first time. Garcia was just one stroke behind the Indian on two under par with two holes to play, but he failed to birdie the 17th and then bogeyed the last to hand the Dubliner the title.

'I went to Valderrama [in 2006] with a tougher chance of winning the Order of Merit, yet I was able to deliver the goods,' Pádraig commented. 'For me, that was a big confidence boost. It signified how far I had come and that I could come into a big event with the pressure on and the focus on, prepare myself right and get it right. I was able to overcome what was usually a tough golf course for me and do the business.

'In many ways I prepared for that event exactly how I would prepare for a major. It was all about getting the best out of that week. I wasn't going in there hoping to play well; I was going in there having to play well and expecting to play well. The interesting thing was that two things happened that week. First of all, getting into contention and achieving my goal was a tremendous boost. But secondly, I played really good golf for sixty-six holes and I had just not got the rewards for it. It was a bit frustrating at that stage because I had played all the golf. But when it was really important my focus kicked in and I just zoned in and holed the putts for the last six holes. And it did teach me a lot. In many ways, that

After a nervous wait with wife, Caroline, and son, Paddy, Pádraig claims the Vardon Trophy, as the 2006 European Tour's Order of Merit leader.

Pádraig holes out on the 72nd during the 2006 Dunlop Phoenix Tournament at the Phoenix Country Club in Mayazaki, Japan, before winning a play-off against Tiger Woods.

mirrored The [2007] Open Championship. It built up and built up, and as it got closer to the end my focus just got sharper and sharper and I got into the zone. It took me sixty-six holes to get into the zone at Valderrama and fifty-four at The Open. But it showed me that if I do the right things, prepare the right way, keep building my game, it might not happen on the first hole but by the end of the tournament it could kick in and I will be in the zone. And as I proved at Valderrama, there is no stopping me when I am in the zone.

'Winning the Order of Merit was a goal of mine, there is no question about that, and it was very satisfying to do it. To go to a golf course that is not a good course for me and produce the goods when it mattered showed me how far I had come since I was going head to head with Goosen. I probably had a more deserved chance of winning the Order of Merit in 2002 because I had been there for longer and played more tournaments during the year. At this one I had come into it at the very end. But it just showed how much I had progressed as a player. At the first one I struggled to get my game in order when the pressure was on; at this one I upped my game when the pressure was on.

'I have got to say that I took tremendous confidence from that. I would say that if any tournament mirrored The Open Championship, Valderrama did because I hit a shot in the water at seventeen as well and got up and down from fifty yards, just like on eighteen at Carnoustie. I hit the shot when I had to; I got my mind focused when I had to. I single-putted my way home. It really showed me that if I am patient, I can get into the zone and anything can happen in that state. When you just have to do it – that's the hardest thing in golf. You can turn up any given week and happen to play well and you can look like the best player in the world. But actually to turn up and play good golf, that's the trick. As Bob Torrance says, "Good players play great when the feeling comes to them. Great players play good when they have to."

'I don't think I have ever been as nervous as when I watched the end of that tournament. It wasn't in my control at that stage. I sat in the players' lounge and I actually couldn't watch. I watched the last hole in The Open and I wasn't nervous at all. But with the Order of Merit there was a finality about it. There was no play-off to look forward to and it was gut-wrenching to watch it. I definitely walked away from that one feeling a few inches taller. I was standing tall just because I did it and things went in my favour. That hasn't always happened to me during my career. I have always said, be patient and things will turn around.'

Torrance's words were still ringing in Pádraig's ears three weeks later when he travelled to Japan to play in the Dunlop Phoenix Tournament and beat Tiger Woods in a play-off to secure his seventeenth professional victory. He erased a three-shot deficit with three birdies over the last six holes to shoot a three-under-par 67 and tie with Woods on nine under par. In the play-off, both men birdied the par-five 18th the first time round, but when they returned a second time Pádraig produced one of the most spectacular birdies of his career to clinch a memorable victory. This time he got lucky after his poor drive ended behind a stunted pine. He decided to thread his ball between a Y-shaped gap formed by the two trunks, and though it caught a part of the tree, it still went forward 120 yards, stopping in a good lie in the rough. He then landed his third shot beyond the hole, using the slope to bring the ball back inside two feet for a tap-in birdie. When Woods missed a twelve-footer, it was all over. With that win, Pádraig joined an élite group of just six players who have beaten Woods when the world number one had held the lead going into the final round.

Pádraig walked away from that event happy that he had added another string to his bow in terms of dealing with pressure down the stretch and producing the goods on demand. 'When you go out to these events there is a bit more hype surrounding you as an international player,' he said. 'There are a lot of expectations. You get a big draw and people are looking at you. Tiger is the big star and I am right in there with him and Shingo Katayama in the last group. Probably what the organizers wanted. And the great thing is that I was a couple of shots behind from the word go and I stuck to my gameplan. I was two behind with four to play and in my head I felt that I had a great chance. Even though it was Tiger

Pádraig finishes the year in great style, receiving help with the champion's jacket from former winner Tiger Woods upon winning the Dunlop Phoenix Tournament after a two-hole play-off.

Woods, I thought, "If I do my thing and play my golf we'll see what happens." I did that, and things turned around in my favour.

'There are two elements to all these wins. One is, I do my thing and then things work out. Secondly, things happen. That really gives you a boost. You think, "Yes, you're on the right track. This is how you tackle things." And there is no question that these wins helped me develop into the player who was able to handle the adversity of the eighteenth at The Open and come out in the play-off and play like I had never hit a bad shot.

'It was helpful that it was Tiger. When you are trying to test out a process of how to do things, it is best when it works against the number one player in the game. It is nice when it works against all comers, but there is nothing better than when it works against Tiger, that's for sure. I walked away from that very pleased that I had a way of handling the situation that worked. Tiger looked like he had it won and he left the door open. When he had a three-shot lead, his game was good at that stage and he had the potential to move on. To my eyes, it looked as though he was thinking, "Par my way home and I will be OK." But I saw the opportunity. That is what was pleasing for me. I am seeing these things and then I am able to respond to them as well.'

A couple of months later, Pádraig lay face down on Dale Richardson's massage table in the locker-room at Sherwood Country Club in Los Angeles. Outside, his caddie Ronan Flood and Dubliner Noel Fox played a game of pool. The balls clacked off each other as they aimlessly whiled away an hour waiting for their friend. Occasionally, the sound of a well-struck shot thumping off the leather pocket liner would reach the inner sanctum where the Australian physiotherapist was working his magic on the Harrington neck.

To his eternal credit, Pádraig is extraordinarily generous with his time, and as inane question followed inane question his patience never appeared to wear as thin as the green baize of the Sherwood Country Club pool table.

'So when was the last time you paid a green fee?' I asked, hopefully. 'Or bought a golf ball?'

'I've never paid a green fee,' came the muffled reply. 'We got free golf when we played on GUI [Golfing Union of Ireland] teams. And I never bought a golf ball – but I sold many.' He lifted his head, and added, 'I went into St Columba's College land and made a dam there. It would silt up and you'd have to drag a club through the silt and rake the balls out. Golf balls were pricey back in the mid-eighties – two [Irish] punts a ball. There was no such thing as cheap golf balls.'

He was in a bit of pain after that, and sensing that the interview was about to come to an abrupt end, I quickly threw in a question about the return to Carnoustie, where he suffered one of the biggest disappointments of his amateur career, losing to Stephen Dundas in the quarter-finals of the 1992 British Amateur Championship. OB on the 18th!

'When you are going to Carnoustie,' Pádraig replied, 'you are going there with a big battle on your hands and I want to prepare properly for it. If the Irish PGA is played the week before, I will certainly be playing if it's on a links course. I want to play links golf that week and I will either be playing social golf on a links or else a tournament. I'd rather play a tournament, and if the PGA is on that week, I'll be there. Any of the links courses would be good, and the European Club would probably be one of the best tests.'

He had other fish to fry before heading down to Brittas Bay the week before The Open, but when he finally turned up at Pat Ruddy's stunning County Wicklow links, Pádraig had grown even more confident about his ability to win a major title. Not only had he finished tied for seventh in the Masters at Augusta, in May he had ended a twenty-five-year wait for a home winner of the Irish Open by seeing off Bradley Dredge of Wales at the first hole of a sudden-death play-off at Adare Manor Hotel and Golf Resort in Limerick.

But it was the Masters that confirmed for Pádraig what he and many had assumed for years – that he was capable of playing the shots to win a major title. Finishing second or third or even seventh didn't come into it. He wanted to win, and had it not been for a 236-yard shot with a hybrid club to the par-five 15th that came within inches of finishing stone dead but instead trickled back into the pond, it might have been a different story. 'Of course I'll be going home thinking, "What if?"' he remarked at the time. 'But I'll also be going home knowing I don't have to change anything to win one of these things. It is not outside the realms of my imagination to win one. I don't have to go home thinking I have to rebuild my golf swing and get to be a better player to win one of these.'

Just two shots off the lead after a birdie at the 12th and an eagle at the 13th, it was the 15th that proved to be his undoing. 'Unfortunately, my Masters finished with probably my best shot of the week. It could have finished stone dead, but that's Augusta. It works out for the winners and the losers are left to rue a few chances missed. When it

Pádraig holes out on the 10th green during the last round of the 2007 Masters, to start a back nine charge, which ended after a second shot into the water on the 15th.

was in the air, it never crossed my mind it would be short. I was actually looking at it in the air and thinking, "I hope it sticks when it hits the green so it doesn't release." When I look back on the tournament, there's the positive that I know I am capable of doing it. And the other positive is that I've again got myself into position, and that's very important. I know I have to be patient and wait for it to be my day. But if I give myself plenty of chances, I'll have more than one day.'

Looking back on that period with the Claret Jug sitting on the kitchen table at home, Pádraig recalled how in fact his Masters performance had had an opposite effect on his game to the one he'd hoped for. Expecting to kick on, instead he fell into a mini slump, finishing tied for forty-third in the Wachovia Championship and a disappointing fifty-second in The Players at Sawgrass. Back in a rut with his game and playing with no spark, his preparation for the Irish Open, a tournament he regards as the fifth major, was hardly ideal.

Yet he felt good as soon as he set foot on the pristine fairways of Adare Manor. From the word go he felt he was going to win. He looked at the golf course and decided it suited him, and as the week wore on there wasn't a moment when he felt he might not win. Even when he lost a three-shot lead and went to the riverside, par-five 18th tied with Dredge, Pádraig never really doubted that he would pull it off. 'I felt it was always within me, that it was my tournament and that I was destined to win it. It was my tournament, and I felt comfortable all the way through. I played good golf and really felt well in control. I know it worked out and it made it exciting in the end. But the tee shot at the eighteenth is very tough and it would be a brave man that would hit that fairway on the day. It was nice to walk away having won your national championship, the fifth-biggest tournament for me. It was definitely a milestone, definitely a goal, and I was over the moon. Thrilled.

'What I'd gained at the other tournaments in knowing what preparation to use, it was all shot to bits for the Irish Open. I had flown

Pádraig plays his third shot to the 18th hole during the play-off for the 2007 Irish Open at Adare Manor, Limerick, which he won after a play-off with Bradley Dredge.

home from the TPC, I was in late and, typically for the Irish Open, I just got nothing done. There are a lot of distractions, and that was the case that week. But what was good for me was that I could overcome that and all those expectations and stresses and perform with a huge hype beforehand that was very similar to a major championship. Before a major the spotlight is shone on your form, what you are doing, the interviews. That is very similar to an Irish Open. With the other events I became comfortable with what works preparation-wise. Then I go into the Irish Open and walk away from it knowing I can handle this extra spotlight, just like a major.

'To me, for the Irish Open, the focus is the same as a major. Maybe even more so. The hardest thing for a professional golfer is to perform on cue. I have said it for years: every guy who wins a tournament is the best player in the world that week. But if you can go to every tournament and play near your best or good golf when you have to, rather than great golf every now and again, that gives you tremendous satisfaction. It gave me satisfaction that I felt good about it, that I felt in position, that I felt I was going to win. There were so many of the emotions that I used in The Open that I carried from other events during the year, feeling that it was my destiny to win this tournament. I am going to win it; there is nothing going to stop me winning it; it is my tournament. I never really thought about the consequences of losing it.

'At The Open, I felt down for a second after I hit my second shot in the water at eighteen and also a second after I holed out and looked at the scoreboard. But at the Irish Open I walked on to the eighteenth tee still thinking I was going to win. I was aware that if Bradley hit the fairway before me, I would have to take that shot on knowing that there was probably a fifty-fifty chance of hitting it in the water. But when he missed the fairway to the right, I was only trying to hit the right edge of the fairway, and even at that I was trying not to hit it left of that. So there was a ninety-five per cent chance of hitting it right and only a five per cent chance of hitting the fairway. There was a moment when Bradley stood on that tee box at the Irish Open and I was thinking, "If he hits this down the middle of the fairway, he is going to put an incredible amount of pressure on me to do the same." It is a very awkward line on the tee box, aiming so far right. To try and aim left you are aiming at the water, not down the left side of the fairway.'

Both men parred the hole, and in the play-off it was Dredge who was first to crack, burying his approach in the bank of the River Maigue. With his mother Breda looking on from behind the 18th green, and with 23,000 fans waiting to hail their hero, Pádraig gave the home crowd what they were looking for.

'After I won I thought, "It's not going to get much better than that this year,"' Pádraig said. 'The interesting thing is that I thought I would really kick on from there, but I didn't at all. Again I stalled. And I stalled again after I won The Open.

John O'Leary, the last
Irishman to win the title
twenty-five years ago,
congratulates Pádraig
after the Irish Open.

Whenever I get on top of things, I don't use confidence very well. Even though it is inside me, I don't use it very well in the immediate aftermath. I don't go on runs of playing well for six or eight weeks. I tend to win, and for some reason – I don't know if it is expectation in my own head or that I try too hard – [winning again] just doesn't happen. And that was very much the case after the Irish Open. As it turned out, it probably worked in my favour because by the time I came to the Irish PGA, I hadn't won and I was expected to win.'

The 2007 Open Championship will be remembered for Pádraig's double-bogey at the 72nd hole, and that remarkable pitch and putt. But Pádraig prefers to remember his seven-iron approach to the first play-off hole, which arguably won him the title. While Sergio Garcia came up well short with his second shot, bouncing off a downslope into a greenside bunker, Pádraig rifled his approach to within ten feet of the flag and walked off the green with a two-stroke lead.

'There is no question that there were shots at The Open that I was better at because I had played links golf at the European Club the week before,' Pádraig said. 'And I would specifically pick that seven iron into the first hole of the play-off. The weather had just turned. The clouds had come in and the temperature had dropped. I had seen from the week before what difference that made to clubbing. I hit a seven iron 162 yards where I would normally have been hitting a seven iron 180 yards that day. That had been brought home to me at the Irish PGA, where the weather and the wind were so difficult and you really had to trust those yardages. Without question, the extra week on a links course helped me out in The Open. And as I only won it in a play-off, it must have won me The Open.'

What Pádraig also discovered at the European Club was that he had the ability to turn on his best stuff when required. Still smiling at the memory, he recalls how he fell two strokes behind Brendan McGovern with six holes of the final round remaining and overheard a snatch of conversation between two elderly gentlemen who were walking up the fairway within a few yards of him. 'You can't beat the spectators on the fairway,' Pádraig said, 'and as I am walking down the thirteenth, one of them turns to the other one and says, "It's really being put up to him, isn't it? We'll see what he's made of now." I stepped by them, and turned and smiled at them. And I went on to birdie the thirteenth, fourteenth and fifteenth to get myself into the lead. It looked like I was going to go three ahead when Brendan got in trouble on the sixteenth, but he made a great five. Then I mess up seventeen and take a seven to be one behind playing the last. I birdie the last and win in a play-off. The best thing about it is that I won €12,500 but it felt as good as any win I have ever had. If I had won by six I would have taken some pleasure out of it too. But I felt great. The way I did it, with birdies, doing it when I had to do it, I felt great.

'I walked into The Open feeling like I had prepared. It wasn't just the physical aspect of playing a week's golf on a links course. I felt that I had outsmarted everybody else in the field by having that four-round competition. The European Club was a great warm-up in that way. It is tight off the tee and it is not as though you can pull out the driver and just hit it. I walked away from it feeling like I was one up on the field and that my preparation had been excellent. And those sorts of things send you into an event with confidence. It was some trip to The Open, and worth every bit of it.'

Harrington left the European Club in a hurry to get to a friend's wedding. Little did he know that he would be having his own celebration just over a week later, where another two burgers would be consumed.

Pádraig celebrates his win in the Irish Open, an event he described as his 'fifth major'.

CHAPTER SIX: JULY 2007

Simply the best

Philip Reid

If destiny's child had been up early on the morning of 16 July, the Monday before the 136th Open Championship, it would have seen two men make their way separately into the Carnoustie Golf Club on Links Parade. It may have been the height of summer, but this was a miserable morning borrowed from the depths of winter. Both Seve Ballesteros and Nick Faldo were suitably waterproofed, allowing them to ignore the heavy rainfall that lashed down on the asphalt pathway as they made their way into the clubhouse at the world's tenth-oldest club for a breakfast briefing that, in an odd Shakespearian way, would have prophetic irony come the defining moments of this latest edition of golf's oldest major.

Pádraig Harrington, who was only just beginning to believe that one day he could win a major, was still in bed. Two days earlier he had won the Irish PGA Championship at the European Club in County Wicklow on Ireland's eastern seaboard, beating Brendan McGovern, a club professional from Headfort Golf Club, in a play-off. Pádraig was enjoying a lie-in ahead of the most hectic week of the year, and would only hear later of six-time major winner Faldo's observations that the current breed of European players were too 'chummy'.

On that Monday, which also marked the official announcement of Ballesteros's retirement from tournament golf, Faldo didn't mince his words. 'It's very different from our era to this era,' he said. 'We were competitors and we were very separate individuals. I always believed you kept your cards close to your chest. Now, the

Opposite Pádraig looks relaxed as he faces questions in his press conference prior to the 2007 Open Championship at Carnoustie, Scotland.

modern guys all have lunch together and then go off to play for a million dollars. And I think, "Hmm, I can't imagine sitting down with Seve or [Greg] Norman or Pricey [Nick Price] before we go out." It all seems very different now. It's quite interesting. They all seem to be so much more chummy. Tiger [Woods] would be the one exception. He won't give away any secrets . . . he's a fierce competitor, and I think that is the difference. We weren't the lads. We were all individuals. Now, it seems like they are the lads. Me, Seve, Langer, Lyle, Woosie. And Ollie [José-María Olázabal] stepped into that group as well . . . look what we achieved. Need I say more? There's eighteen majors between six guys. That's eighteen majors to zero!'

In any given week, the caddy shack harbours more storytellers than a novelists' convention. It didn't take long for Faldo's comments to find their way to the range, where players and caddies alike devoured the words like hungry fishwives starved of gossip. Pádraig was just one of the players to absorb them. And so, on the Tuesday during his official press conference to the assembled media from around the world, he gave his response to Faldo's genuinely spoken words. It provided an interesting insight into his own world. 'We all have different ways of going about our things,' he said. 'Just because you're a nice guy, it doesn't mean you can't win a major. You have to have an instinct to win, but nice guys do win!'

Pádraig had arrived in Carnoustie with two wins already secured in 2007. In May, at Adare Manor, he had become the first Irishman since John O'Leary to win the Irish Open; and the previous week, while most players competed in the Barclays Scottish Open at Loch Lomond – a beautiful lakeside course but vastly different from the nuances of links golf – he had competed and won, again in a play-off, in the Irish PGA. But he'd missed the cut at the last major the previous month, the US Open at Oakmont, where Angel Cabrera became the second first-time major winner of the year (Zach Johnson was the first, at the US Masters).

Still, going into Carnoustie, Pádraig was due a good performance in a British Open. Since his fifth-place finish at Muirfield in 2002, when he was only a shot outside a four-way play-off eventually won by Ernie Els, Pádraig's record read twenty-second (2003), missed the cut (2004), didn't play because of the death of his father (2005), and missed the cut (2006). There was a sense of expectancy about this Open Championship. According to the bookmakers, Pádraig Harrington was rated as fourth favourite, at odds that were generally available at 22–1, mainly because he had won the Alfred Dunhill Links Championship – partly played on the Carnoustie links – twice in the previous four years. An accountant in spirit and by qualification, Pádraig understood the odds but disputed that the competition represented his best chance of winning a major. On that Tuesday in Carnoustie, two days before the first ball of the 136th Open Championship was struck, he commented, 'I wouldn't accept it's my best chance of winning . . . sure

I look forward to coming here, but I can't have that ultimatum in my head that this is my best chance. That's going to put too much expectation on the week, too much focus on the week. I just have to keep working on a numbers game, to keep playing and to keep getting myself into contention. Just because I've won here before [in the Dunhill], I can't say it is my big chance. Having an attitude like that will only put more pressure on yourself. The key is to tone it down all the way, and just play to get yourself into position with nine holes to go on Sunday.'

During most majors it is customary to find Pádraig Harrington playing practice rounds with his fellow Ryder Cupper Paul McGinley. Although both players hailed from the same suburb of Rathfarnham in Dublin, had played for the same GAA Club at Ballyboden St Endas and, in amateur golf, had played on the same Walker Cup team at Portmarnock in 1991, there was a near five-year age gap between them and their friendship had only really grown while out on tour as professionals. Since winning the World Cup for Ireland in 1997 at Kiawah Island it seemed as if they were joined at the hip. In 2006, each had been awarded an honorary doctorate in a ceremony at the National University of Ireland, Maynooth. And, coincidentally in light of Nick Faldo's pre-tournament comments, it was a little ironic that Pádraig should have only recently gone out of his way to get McGinley together with Dr Bob Rotella, the famed sports psychologist who had been his mental guru for the best part of a decade. For Pádraig, friendship was more important than any rivalry. If he could help McGinley, he would.

Pádraig compares notes with friend Paul McGinley during a practice round at Carnoustie, a round during which he was 9 under par for a twelve-hole stretch.

On the Wednesday afternoon, the eve of The Open, Pádraig and McGinley bypassed the 1st hole at Carnoustie – a par four of 406 yards with out of bounds all down the left – and started their final practice round on the 2nd. Pádraig's form over the first few holes was nothing to write home about; anyone watching would have kept their money in their pockets rather than venture down to the bookmakers. He parred the 2nd, bogeyed the 3rd and then ran up a quadruple-bogey on the 4th, where he found a fairway bunker and did an impersonation of the man from the Hamlet ad.

What happened thereafter, though, was the first real indication that this could indeed be his week. From the 5th to the 9th holes, he had two birdies and three pars. Good, but nothing spectacular. It was only after he turned for home that he produced the type of fireworks that players

often wish could be kept for tournament rounds and not wasted in practice. Over the next seven holes, he went birdie-birdie-par-birdie-eagle-birdie-birdie. Pádraig had got into the zone. He felt good; but, rather than broadcast his deeds from the rooftops, he managed to keep it quiet. After all, the Dubliner had been around long enough to know that birdies and eagles in practice don't count at the end of the day. Still, at least he could go to bed that night knowing that if he'd found the zone once, he could do it again.

Pádraig plays an iron to the 2nd hole during his first round of 69 (2 under par) at Carnoustie. The ball finished in a greenside bunker, forcing him to play out left-handed. Pádraig finished the day tied for eighth place.

The first shots of The Open Championship of 2007 at Carnoustie were struck at 6.30 a.m. on Thursday, 19 July. Only a handful of spectators were on hand to witness Joe Durant, Oliver Wilson and Ben Bunny depart the 1st tee in the quest for the famed Claret Jug. Almost seven hours later, at 1.20 p.m., Pádraig Harrington started his own personal journey in search of fulfilment. Richie Ramsay, a young Scottish amateur who had won the US Amateur and was on the cusp of a move into the professional ranks, and David Toms, a likeable American familiar to Pádraig from Ryder Cup matches, made up the three-ball.

Back in 1999, when Scotland's Paul Lawrie won The Open at Carnoustie, the rough was impossibly heavy. For anyone who cared to look, players competing in The Open's return to the august venue were reminded of that carnage by photographs that lined the corridor walls of the hotel behind the 1st and 18th holes. One in particular offered a graphic reminder. It showed the scoreboard of one group that had completed the second round, which read: 'SINGH +19 MEDIATE +13 GARCIA +30'. Whether they liked it or not, the woes of Vijay Singh, Rocco Mediate and Sergio Garcia were offered to anyone who cared to stop to peer at the image.

As if to prove that the past was the past, Sergio Garcia found a measure of redemption in his first-round play that Thursday, when yet more rain had taken the fire out of the Carnoustie links. Using his belly-putter to terrific effect, the Spaniard, who had walked away from Carnoustie in tears eight years earlier after missing the halfway cut and finishing at the tail-end of the field, shot a brilliant opening-round 65 – six under par – that left him alone at the top of the leaderboard. In fact, as if to back up the Royal and Ancient commitment to making this Open a fair test of golf, no fewer than twenty-four players managed to better par on that first day, among them Rory McIlroy, an eighteen-year-old teenager from Holywood in County Down, Northern Ireland, who had earned his place in the championship courtesy of his win in the 2006 European Amateur Strokeplay Championship. McIlroy shot a 68 and was tied third, one stroke behind McGinley and one better than Pádraig.

Garcia's round, though, was the best of all. Vijay Singh had been advising Garcia for the best part of a year that he should try using a belly-putter, and there was a measure of satisfaction in his voice after he shot into the lead. 'This is not about revenge for me,' observed the Spaniard, who had improved by twenty-four strokes his second-round 89 from 1999. 'I just want to play solid. This is a good start, definitely what the doctor ordered.'

Pádraig, too, was happy with his lot. He had broken his driver two weeks earlier during a practice round on the eve of the Smurfit Kappa European Open and was still not entirely happy with his replacement, an old driver with seven and a half degrees of loft that had been brought back to life for the links conditions. Despite concerns about his driving, a first-round 69 left him well in contention, on the same score as world number one Tiger Woods, who had finished runner-up in the first two majors of the year, to Johnson at the Masters and to Cabrera at the US Open.

In that first round, Pádraig's best shot, strangely enough, was not for a birdie. It came on the 2nd hole, where he put his approach into a greenside bunker. He had a horrible lie right under the lip, so horrible that many players would have considered the option of taking an unplayable lie in the bunker. Not Pádraig Harrington. He took a sand wedge from caddie Ronan Flood, turned the face round and played out left-handed. It was a brave shot that magically found its way on to the putting surface and provided more than a hint that the Irishman was up for the challenge.

Back in the clubhouse, Pádraig felt that 69 was a good return. 'I'm pleased with it. I've just got to do more of the same [for another three days] . . . I didn't drive the ball as well as I wanted to, so that is something to concern me.' But he had his game face on, and that focused look spoke louder than any words.

To win a major, a player must connect four links in a chain. After Friday's second round of The Open, Sergio Garcia had completed half of the task, having crafted shots, holed putts and avoided calamity to claim the midway lead. There was a pep in his step as he made his way from green to tee, his engaging smile hinting that perhaps he had served his apprenticeship and that his time was beckoning. The tears of 1999 were long gone.

During that second round a fresh breeze came in off the North Sea, and the challenge for the players was further accentuated by some shrewd pin placements

A missed putt at the 2nd hole during a second round of 73 (2 over par) at Carnoustie, left Pádraig tied thirteenth place at the halfway stage.

by the R&A; there was as a result a heavy price to pay for impetuousness. Garcia remained immune from any such disasters in his round of 71, for a six-under-par 136, which gave him a two-stroke lead at the halfway stage of The Open over Korea's K. J. Choi.

Not everybody had steered clear of trouble. Tiger Woods had incurred the wrath of the course as early as his first tee shot, snap-hooking his ball into the burn down the left-hand side of the fairway. Pádraig Harrington's woes were reserved for the closing hole, a par four of 499 yards where the Barry Burn sneaked its way one way and another up and across the fairway and in front of the green. His problems had nothing to do with the burn, however, rather with a poor drive and a poor touch with the putter in hand. On that 18th hole, the Dubliner – right in the thick of the action – somehow ran up a six that left him signing for a 73. On Friday evening he found himself six strokes adrift of Garcia on 142, level par.

His problems on the 18th had begun on the tee, where his drive was so far right that it crossed the Barry Burn and finished up in the rough beside the 17th fairway. Of course, it could have been worse: the ball might actually have gone into the water hazard. But it was not a place from where the green was accessible in two. All Pádraig could do was lay up and play back on to the fairway. He gave himself a chance of a fighting par by putting his approach to twenty feet, only to follow up with heavy-handed putting for what seemed to be a costly double-bogey.

Within minutes of signing his card, Pádraig – whose sports psychologist Dr Bob Rotella had stayed with him in the rented house in Carnoustie all week, which proved to be a good move – had already erased the three-putt from his mind. 'That six is not going to affect the outcome of this tournament for me,' he insisted. 'I don't want to be too far behind but it just means that I go out and play good golf for the weekend. That's it. There's a lot of golf left in this tournament and maybe I'll go out with a little more aggression from now on. There are thirty-six holes left, and whether I'm one under or two under or level par, it doesn't make any difference to my chances on the weekend.'

For Garcia, there were no thoughts of having to play catch-up. On that Friday afternoon, the midway leader contemplated what it meant to be leading The Open Championship. 'I'd rather be leading than be eight shots back, that's for sure, because you don't feel like you have to push your game to the limit all the time,' he said.

On Saturday evening, Garcia was still leading, though he would have done well to consider the advice once offered to anyone who cared to listen by Sir Winston Churchill: 'It is a mistake to try to look too far ahead. The chain of destiny can only be grasped one link at a time.' A 68 had left the Spaniard on 204, nine under par. Steve Stricker, the American who had enjoyed a fine summer, had run into second place on his own after a third-round 64, while Pádraig's 68 enabled him to move into a group of seven players that also included Paul McGinley in third place, six shots behind Garcia.

Could Pádraig win from there on the final day?

Pádraig lines up a putt on the 12th hole during the third round. A round of 68 (3 under par) left Pádraig tied third and six shots behind leader Sergio Garcia with a round to play.

That Saturday evening he arrived at the putting green. His demeanour was one that indicated he was totally relaxed with himself, but his words were cautionary. 'A 68 is a nice return, but it is not quite good enough to get right in there. It has left it in Sergio's hands . . . but I do feel I have a low round in me. I have to stay patient and let it happen.' And an unusual thing happened after that: Pádraig, a range rat with the reputation of spending more time on the practice ground than just about any other player in the game, decided that there was no need for any further work. It was an arrangement he had come to with his caddie, Ronan Flood. It was simple: if Pádraig was playing well enough to win, they would avoid the sound of ball hitting titanium ad nauseam on the range.

Later that night, in the house in Carnoustie where he was staying with his family and back-up team, Pádraig made what at first was a casual remark. 'I'm going to win,' he said. It was designed to ignite a reaction from his listeners, so that he could gauge it. But to him, it was more than that. It was part of the mental imaging Rotella had encouraged him to put into the right side of his brain.

'I'm going to win,' he said. 'This is it.'

Sports psychologist and Open week house-guest, Bob Rotella, has worked with Pádraig for ten years.

If Pádraig Harrington went to bed the night before the final round of the 136th Open Championship having instilled extra belief into the right side of his brain about his prospects of laying hands on the old Claret Jug, such favourable thoughts were knocked in the early hours of Sunday, 22 July, when he woke up with a strain in his neck.

Ever since the US PGA Championship at Hazeltine in 2002, when his physical therapist, Dale Richardson, was forced to conduct remedial action on a neck injury shortly after the player had literally tapped his opening shot on the first hole of the third round about 120 yards off the tee, Pádraig had at various times sought to overcome a recurring C5 disc weakness in his vertebrae. A new physical regime had enabled him to strengthen the muscles around the joint, but there were still times when the old injury flared up. Waking up in the middle of the night just hours before the final round of the 2007 Open was not what the doctor ordered.

Pádraig propped himself up with pillows so as to limit any movement and reduce the risk of aggravating things. Pretty soon, he fell back into a sleep from which he would not emerge until ten o'clock the following morning, some four hours before his scheduled tee-time in the third-last group. Normally he likes to get up two and a half hours (plus travelling time) before a scheduled tee-time. However, the late two o'clock start meant he could take things at his leisure that Sunday morning.

By the time he arrived at the breakfast table, Ronan Flood had already departed for the course to scout the final day's pin placements; but Jonny Smith, the soon-to-be husband of the Harringtons' nanny, was sitting there with half a dozen golf balls idly placed in front of him. Knowing that Flood had already packed the customary dozen balls for his bag, Pádraig wondered why the extra balls were on the table. Then the reality dawned on him.

'Ronan has put them out for the play-off, hasn't he?' he said.

Pádraig was right: Flood had phoned to ask Smith to get another six balls, just in case they were needed for a play-off. This gesture of faith, such as it was at the time, was appreciated by Pádraig. It reminded him that Nick Faldo had come from six shots behind Greg Norman on the last day of the 1996 US Masters, and that Paul Lawrie had come from ten behind in the 1999 British Open at Carnoustie. As any golfer knows, it can be difficult to make up such ground if there is a logjam of players to the leader. But when only one – in this case Steve Stricker – lies between the chasing posse and the leader, anything is possible. Pádraig tucked into his scrambled eggs and toast with renewed vigour.

The house he had rented for the week in Carnoustie was only five minutes from the golf course. He arrived at the links at 12.15 p.m., and the first thing he did was to receive physio treatment from Dale Richardson. He had already conducted his own warm-up regime in the house, so the physio visit had as much to do with having a feel-good chat as with getting ready to hit balls on the range.

After almost twenty minutes of standard physiotherapy, and with no indication that the neck spasm that had woken him up so rudely was any cause for concern, Pádraig headed for the range. It was 12.40, but the extra time allowed him to stop and sign autographs and paraphernalia for spectators who had ignored the early-morning rain to descend on the course in their thousands.

On the range, Pádraig went through his routine with coach Bob Torrance. 'I hit a few shots, but I didn't stand on the range and think, "Wow, this is the best I've ever hit the golf ball,"' he commented. 'The focus was much more on getting my head ready than getting my swing ready.' After about half an hour he headed for the short-game practice area, where he hit a few bunker shots and a number of chip shots. He arrived at the putting green only twelve minutes before his scheduled two o'clock tee-time, spent seven minutes putting, and then made his way to the 1st tee, where he arrived with four minutes to spare. He couldn't but notice the large Irish tricolour and a group of fans located in the grandstand to the left of the fairway.

Once on the tee, Pádraig tied his shoelaces, as he always does. It is not superstition, just a habit he has always had. 'There's no point wearing a good pair of golf shoes unless they're comfortable,' he says. 'I always retie the laces to make sure the shoe is fitting tightly.' Laces tied, Pádraig, still generally available at 20–1

with bookmakers, turned to Flood and requested his five wood. It was an aggressive play off the 1st tee, given the huge fairway bunker positioned at the 260-yard mark, but it was a statement of intent.

Providing an omen, perhaps, the weather shifted shortly before Pádraig and the late starters teed off. The day had started with heavy and consistent rain which left fairways saturated and a number of bunkers flooded; greenstaff were forced to revert to the old ways of using buckets to bail out water from the sand traps. Just before Pádraig, in the third from last pairing, began his round, the sun broke through the grey clouds.

The rain took the fire out of the Carnoustie links, while the R&A had opted for realistic pin placements to give players chances of making a final-day charge. So it was that Richard Green leapfrogged through the field with a 64, while Ben Curtis and Hunter Mahan shot 65s. Those scores served to remind those late starters that there were birdies – and eagles – to be made.

Crucially, despite an early birdie on the 3rd, Garcia failed to take advantage. Ernie Els threatened to make a run, only to stumble over the closing stretch of holes, probably the toughest in championship golf. The surprise gatecrasher proved to be Argentina's Andres Romero, who produced a truly unbelievable round which featured no fewer than ten birdies. But he also suffered two double-bogeys. The first, when his approach to the 12th green finished in a bush, seemed at the time to have stopped his charge. Rather than capitulating, however, the Argentine's response was to birdie the next four holes. His putter was like a magic wand; he couldn't miss. Then disaster struck on the par-four 17th, where Romero got greedy with his second shot out of rough. Using a two iron, he shanked the ball into the concrete wall of the Barry Burn and watched in disbelief as it skitted across the 18th fairway and finished up out of bounds. That wicked slice of bad luck led to his second double-bogey six, and he followed that with a bogey on the last to finish alone in third.

Romero's demise left the way clear for Pádraig, who had made serious inroads into Garcia's lead. The Irishman's gameplan had been to push for early birdies, and while Garcia covered the front nine in thirty-eight strokes including three bogeys as his belly-putter finally neglected him, Pádraig completed the same stretch in thirty-three strokes, claiming birdies at the 3rd, 6th and 9th holes without dropping a shot. When he birdied the 11th, the starting deficit had been erased. The chase was over and he was playing for a different prize, one he had always dreamed of.

Pádraig and Flood had made a pact with each other prior to the start of the round. There would be no looking at leaderboards, no updates about who was doing what elsewhere. They agreed that the first strategic decision would come on the par-five 14th. If Pádraig needed birdies, Flood would hand him a driver; if he was in the thick of things, he would be given a five wood for safety. When the two reached the 14th tee, Flood produced a five wood from the bag. Pádraig knew what it meant.

The key shot of The Open Championship – Pádraig plays his fifth shot to the 72nd hole, to five feet from the hole.

The 14th hole is a par five of 514 yards. Up to then, Pádraig had played brilliantly but hadn't got a real break. On the 12th his putt had looked destined to fall into the tin cup, only to lip out. On the 13th another birdie putt stopped on the edge and refused to drop. So he believed the golfing gods owed him one when his second shot to the 14th got a kindly kick out of greenside rough and rolled on to the putting surface. He knocked in the eagle putt to get to nine under. He was leading The Open.

Garcia's response to this move was to claim back-to-back birdies on the 13th and 14th, to reach nine under. But when he dropped a shot on the 15th after taking a conservative play off the tee and failing to reach the green in two, it meant that Pádraig, as he stood with driver in hand on the 18th tee, was again leading the championship.

What happened next was unforgettable. Pádraig's drive went right, towards the Barry Burn. For a moment it seemed that luck would side with him as the ball ran along the pedestrian bridge, but it only teased and tantalized those with hearts in their mouths before falling into the hazard. Memories of Jean van de Velde's flirtation with the Claret Jug in 1999 filled spectators' minds.

After taking a drop, Pádraig's approach of 229 yards to the green was caught a little heavy. From the moment of impact he knew it would not reach its destination. The ball took two bounces, then fell into the same burn which meanders its way up the fairway before running in front of the green. In the end, Pádraig showed his fortitude by making a fabulous up and down from forty-eight yards off a tight lie over the burn for what turned out to be a fine double-bogey six.

It meant, however, that Garcia was one stroke clear as he prepared to play the 18th. But the Spaniard, too, faltered with the great prize in sight. His cautious play off the tee left him with some 250 yards to the green, and his approach found the front left greenside bunker, from where he splashed out to twelve feet. He still had a putt to win The Open; and for all the world it looked like a great putt. But it didn't drop into the tin cup. Garcia's 73 to Pádraig's 67 meant the two had finished locked together on 277, seven under par. A four-hole play-off would now determine who got his hands on the Claret Jug.

Pádraig Harrington watched Garcia's missed par putt on a television monitor in the recorders' hut. Having finished his round with that double-bogey on the 18th, the Irishman had allowed himself a first glance at the giant scoreboard that dominated the roadside grandstand by the finishing green. In that glance he believed he had allowed the Claret Jug to slip from his grasp.

His desperation, though, was short-lived: he was rescued from his own thoughts by his three-year-old son Paddy, who ran on to the green to innocently congratulate him. In that moment, Pádraig readjusted, saluted the generous ovation of the crowd and made his way to sign his card. In checking and double-checking it, and then signing for a 67, he realized just how well he had played. When Garcia missed his putt for par, any pessimism that had infiltrated his mindset was banished. After all, despite the shenanigans on the last hole, he, not Garcia, had played the best golf that Sunday.

As one, Pádraig and Flood rose from their seats in the recorders' hut and re-emerged for the play-off over the 1st, 16th, 17th and 18th holes. Who would follow in the footsteps of former winners at Carnoustie, men like Tommy Armour in 1931; Henry Cotton in 1937; Ben Hogan, affectionately dubbed the 'Wee Ice

Mon' by the Scots, in 1953; Gary Player in 1968; and Tom Watson in 1975? That was Carnoustie's last Open until 1999, when Paul Lawrie triumphed in a play-off with Justin Leonard and Jean van de Velde, who had infamously taken a triple-bogey seven on the 18th when a double-bogey would have won him the title. Pádraig's antics on the 18th in regulation had threatened to surpass those of van de Velde, but the Irishman had rescued a six despite twice being in the water. Given a second chance, he was determined there would be no further slip-ups.

The first hole at Carnoustie is a par four of 406 yards and is known simply as 'Cup'. When Ben Hogan won the Claret Jug on the links in 1953, he hit a two-iron approach shot. Times have changed. When Pádraig hit a five wood off the tee, he had no more than a seven iron in his hand for a shot that would help shape his destiny.

While Garcia's approach found a semi-plugged lie in a greenside bunker, from which he failed to save par, Pádraig's approach attracted wild enthusiasm from those by the green as it rolled up to ten feet from the hole. It was on a similar line to the putt Pádraig had taken, and missed, on his opening hole of the final round over five hours earlier. And despite all that had happened in the ensuing time, he remembered that it was a straighter putt than it appeared. He stayed true to his conviction, picked a line on the left lip, and rolled in the birdie putt. After the first hole he moved two shots clear of the Spaniard.

On the 16th, a par three called 'Barry Burn', Pádraig pulled out his utility club but missed the green to the left. The ball finished in a swale. Garcia added to the drama, actually hitting the flagstick with his tee shot, only for the ball to finish eighteen feet from the hole. Pádraig made a great up-and-down to save par, while Garcia missed his birdie putt. The status quo remained: Pádraig Harrington was two shots up with two holes to play.

The two finishing holes at Carnoustie are no ordinary holes. The 17th, called 'Island' after the fact that the landing area on the fairway is just that, surrounded as it is on either side by the burn, is a par four of 461 yards, while the 18th, in Pádraig's reckoning, is the toughest finishing hole in championship golf. Both men parred the 17th, then turned to the 18th, a par four of 499 yards known as 'Hope'. Not much more than an hour earlier the two had met on the bridge over Barry Burn, Garcia as he walked down the 17th fairway, Pádraig as he walked across to assess his playing options having put his drive into the water hazard. This time, Pádraig had no intention of using the driver again. Now, two shots clear of his rival, the only option off the tee was a conservative one. He effectively played the hole as a par five, finding the fairway off the tee with his favoured utility club and laying up short of the burn with his approach. From there, he hit his approach over the water to thirty feet from the hole, two-putted for a bogey five and, proving that nice guys do win, claimed the Claret Jug.

Epilogue

I have learned through the years to savour my victories and so I now celebrate a lot more then I did in my early career. It is important to celebrate the wins as it helps you to remember them and want them more and more. It was no different with The Open.

I had a great week immediately after the victory, with a number of parties and appearances, including taking the trophy to Stackstown Golf Club on the Monday evening, which coincided with the prizegiving of the Tylestyle Trophy, a junior open competition, which was my first team win at the age of thirteen. This was followed by an all-night party at the Sporting Emporium in Dublin, which a number of family members, friends and those who have helped me during my career attended. Later in the week I was officially congratulated by the Taoiseach and the Minister for Sport at the Government Buildings in Dublin.

Since winning The Open, I have sought the advice of a number of other major winners about their experiences. I have noted that for many of the one-time winners, the biggest challenge for them is to maintain their game beyond what naturally feels like the pinnacle of their career.

The same applies to me – winning The Open has been a personal dream. However, I must now set clear goals for myself to keep my focus going forward (I keep these to myself so as not to be judged on them by anyone), but I can say that I now want to build on this success and become the best player I possibly can.

It was evident to me after my win that I couldn't wait to play my next major – when you taste success at this level you feel like nothing else compares to it. But I also realize that there are many more tournaments and in order to be ready for a major you must tackle every shot of every round of every tournament like it's the most important shot you are ever going to hit. It is the ability to shoot 74 instead of 75 or finish thirty-ninth instead of fortieth that makes you sharp and ready to play on the big stage of a major.

Hopefully this means that I will contend in many more majors and secure more titles. I may or may not succeed in winning another; however, if the latter turns out to be the case, it will certainly not be through lack of effort.

With a wonderful family and another child on the way, I feel extremely privileged to be in the position I am. How many of us get paid to do something we love so much? I do appreciate, however, that there are others who are less fortunate. With this in mind I established the Pádraig Harrington Charitable Foundation, which provides financial assistance to deserving beneficiaries throughout Ireland and the rest of the world.

In conclusion, I would sincerely hope to be an example to others in following their dreams. As my old coach Howard Bennett used to say, the 'three Ds' of dedication, discipline and desire can overcome any obstacle.

If my legacy could be to provide inspiration to others, this would evoke greater pride in my dad than winning any trophy.

Pádraig Harrington
October 2007

Pádraig's Open Notes

LITTLE-KNOWN FACTS

1 • I changed Wilson drivers three times during the week, from a 9° loft version in practice, 7.5° on Thursday and Friday, to 8.5° on Saturday and Sunday. The latter driver was used to drive on the 72nd hole and is still in the bag.

2 • I strained my neck on Monday morning, couldn't practise and needed continuous physio throughout the week.

3 • My family and I stayed in Poppy House, normally a B&B in Carnoustie.

4 • My first drink out of the Claret Jug was John Smith's Extra Smooth bitter, as a promise to my manager.

5 • I had lost two play-offs to Sergio before The Open.

6 • This year was the first time that Ronan, my caddie, made the weekend at The Open.

7 • We purchased balls in the Pro Shop for the play-off as initially we couldn't find the person who had our reserves. However, they were located just before we teed off.

8 • My best hole during the week was the tough par-4 9th hole, which I played in 2 under par.

9 • My caddie believed that the 17th was my best hole during the week, because I was never out of position on what is a difficult hole.

10 • Up until the Thursday morning I had not set foot on the practice putting green, with a maximum of ten minutes before each tournament round and the play-off, which indicated that I was trusting my putting stroke during the week.

KEY SHOTS

1ST ROUND

2ND HOLE	Left-handed shot from a greenside bunker to 20 feet
18TH HOLE	48-yard bunker shot into wind that nearly went in before spinning back to 4 feet

2ND ROUND

8TH HOLE	Soft lob shot over a bunker from a tight lie to one foot. My shot of the week

3RD ROUND

13TH HOLE	Long chip from way right of the green to one foot, after an ugly tee shot

4TH ROUND

3RD HOLE	51-yard pitch off a downslope to one foot, producing my first birdie of the day
5TH HOLE	Chip over a bunker up a tier in the green, stone dead
9TH HOLE	6 iron to 8 feet, producing the birdie that got my round going
11TH HOLE	8 iron to 3 feet, birdie
14TH HOLE	Putt for eagle. The excitement of which required me to calm myself down
15TH HOLE	5 wood tee shot, which I felt was the toughest tee shot on the course
16TH HOLE	Hybrid club to 5 feet
18TH HOLE	Pitch from 48 yards to 5 feet
18TH HOLE	5-foot putt for par to get into the play-off
1ST PLAY-OFF	5 wood tee shot down the middle. I didn't know what to expect after the last few shots of regular play
1ST PLAY-OFF	7 iron to 10 feet, birdie
2ND PLAY-OFF	First putt up the bank, where I had to really trust my feel
3RD PLAY-OFF	4 iron to 5 feet
4TH PLAY-OFF	Putt to win!